CONTENTS

ISTANBUL REVISITED

Three-nil down in the biggest club game of the season, many Liverpool fans' hopes at half-time in the 2005 UEFA Champions League final in Istanbul centred purely on damage limitation.

However, once a rousing rendition of You'll Never Walk Alone at the Ataturk Stadium restored a sense of pride, a goal from captain Steven Gerrard early in the second-half provided the catalyst for one of the most incredible turnarounds in the history of the European Cup.

As we celebrate the 20th anniversary, this is a reflection on one of the most incredible nights in the storied history of Liverpool FC.

From the route to the final to fans' journeys and celebrations and the thoughts of the main players themselves, this is a trip back in time that no Kopite will ever want to forget.

Three goals in six minutes, Jerzy Dudek's heroics, the prssure of penalties and Gerrard hoisting the cup aloft in the early hours of the following morning, Turkish time - this souvenir celebration recaps all the key moments.

We also hear from commentator Clive Tyldesley who provided the soundtrack for many Reds fans watching around the globe and who must have sensed something in the air when he greeted Gerrard's header with the words: 'Hello, hello! Here we go!'

We also highlight mementos and memorabilia of the night and look at some Istanbul-related moments you have missed at the time and some that may have passed you by since.

Featuring stunning imagery, fascinating archive interviews with the matchday programme and magazine plus modern-day analysis, this is a celebration of the night Liverpool FC won the European Cup for keeps.

Damage limitation? In Istanbul, we won it five times!

 @lfc  @liverpoolfc   liverpoolfc   @liverpoolfc   @liverpoolfc

Reach Sport

Editor William Hughes **Writers** Chris McLoughlin, David Cottrell **Production Editor** Michael McGuinness **Art Editor & Cover Design** Colin Sumpter **Design** Colin Sumpter, Chris Collins, Jonah Webb **Marketing & Communications Manager** Claire Brown **Thanks to** Mark Platt, Andy Marsden **Photography** Alamy, Mirrorpix, Liverpool Echo, John Powell, Andrew Powell, Nicholas Taylor, Nikki Dyer © Liverpool Football Club & Athletic Grounds Ltd Published by **Reach Sport** www.reachsportshop.com **Printed by** Buxton Press

NOTHING COMES CLOSE TO
istanbul

*Two decades on, DAVID COTTRELL examines the legacy of
Liverpool's remarkable victory at the Ataturk Stadium*

The French sports paper which kicked off what we now know as the UEFA Champions League currently has a special publication on sale. Entitled **70 ANS DE C1** – L'Equipe has always called it 'C1' for short – it celebrates the most legendary matches in the competition's history since it all started back in 1955.

On the front cover the famous trophy is surrounded by nine players, all previous winners, in their prime: Alfredo Di Stefano, Eusebio, Johan Cruyff, Basile Boli, Manuel Neuer, Cristiano Ronaldo, Lionel Messi, Paolo Maldini...and Steven Gerrard.

You'd expect Liverpool to feature prominently inside and they do. There's a page of course for the 2019 semi-final versus Barcelona and another for the 1977 quarter-final with French side Saint-Etienne. A whole spread, though, is devoted to the 2005 final against AC Milan. The report begins like this...

We have never forgotten the colour of that night. It was red. We have never forgotten the half-time 'You'll Never Walk Alone' at the Atatürk Stadium. It was like a prayer. We have never forgotten the seven minutes (6:43, to be exact) during which Liverpool came back from 0-3 to 3-3 on May 25, 2005, in Istanbul, in the Champions League final. We cannot forget magical nights and miracles.

'The colour of that night'. How wonderfully evocative and still dreamily true 20 years on. For those who were there, even through the wonky parallax of hindsight, it's hard to recall Istanbul without a rose-tinted filter: the shirts, scarves, hats, caps and banners brought by tens of thousands of fans dressed more for a beach holiday than a distinctly chilly venue 20 miles west of the city-centre; the official programme cover, match tickets and all the rest of the tournament paraphernalia; the ubiquitous Turkish national flag waved by local youngsters who ran alongside the convoy bussing supporters to the ground, having taken Liverpool joyously to their hearts. Was there even a touch of red in the gleaming alloy of the trophy? It felt like it.

Istanbul's tall tales and campfire stories are told elsewhere in this publication. But what about its legacy over the last two decades and counting?

Over the last half-century Liverpool's relationship with Europe's premier competition is broadly characterised by three eras. The Paisley/Fagan campaigns of 1976 to 1985, when only domestic champions qualified and competed, yielded four triumphs but culminated in a devastating disaster. The millennium brought a Houllier/Benitez renaissance between 2001 and 2009 which returned the Reds to the top table on a regular basis but saw them cross paths with nouveau riche Chelsea too many times. Now the modern love affair with the Champions League, kindled first by Brendan Rodgers then Jürgen Klopp, continues under Arne Slot.

"For those who were there, even through the wonky parallax of hindsight, it's hard to recall Istanbul without a rose-tinted filter: the shirts, scarves, hats, caps and banners brought by tens of thousands of fans dressed more for a beach holiday than a distinctly chilly venue 20 miles west of the city-centre"

If the 2005 win was a rehabilitation of sorts among the Continent's elite after so long on the outside looking in – heralding as it did a spell of regular Champions League participation in which the Reds reached another final, a semi-final and a quarter-final – the manner of victory only added to the club's aura and allure. We'd won it five times.

It meant that Liverpool could attract a rising star of the calibre of Fernando Torres in the summer of 2007. It must have played into Fenway Sports Group's thinking in the autumn of 2010 that there was something different about this football club, something special, despite a perilous period on and off the pitch. Surely it helped entice Klopp to end his self-imposed sabbatical from football in 2015, a decade after the dust and red ticker-tape at the Ataturk had settled, and lead Liverpool back to the promised land. "For me, it fits perfect," he said upon his appointment as manager. "Just the right type of guy [for LFC]," said Klopp's former chairman at Mainz, citing emotion as the common denominator between club, manager and fans.

Ahead of the group-stage reunion with Milan in the 2021/22 tournament, Klopp was asked to think back to Istanbul – back then as a 37-year-old he'd just managed Mainz to eleventh place in their first-ever Bundesliga season – and admitted: "That night I was thinking about not watching the second half, to be honest, because like everybody in the world – apart from a few people

"This writer, like so many fans, has his little stash of 2005 memorabilia: travel documents and boarding passes from the earlier round-by-round trips to Leverkusen, Turin and West London; a set of 12 unused postcards of Istanbul and some grainy Taksim Square photos taken on a disposable camera"

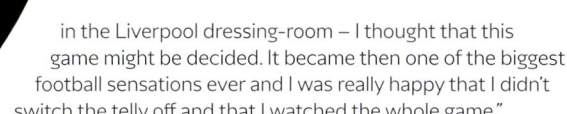

in the Liverpool dressing-room – I thought that this game might be decided. It became then one of the biggest football sensations ever and I was really happy that I didn't switch the telly off and that I watched the whole game."

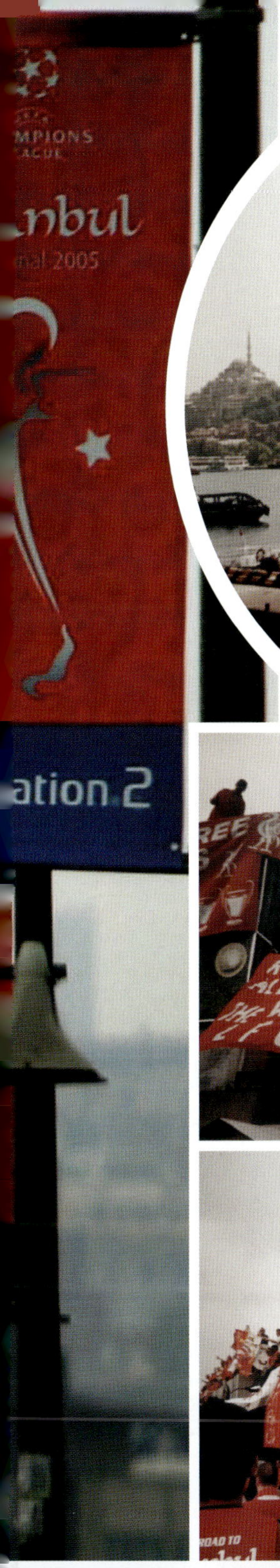

Elsewhere Istanbul resonated so much in the mind of a 13-year-old Mohamed Salah that the Reds were his team of choice when he played FIFA on his console. "It was special to me even though I was very young," he revealed to France Football magazine. "I always had Liverpool and I always used to put Steven Gerrard upfront because he had a great shot. Then I had Jerzy Dudek in goal and Jamie Carragher and Sami Hyypia in defence."

'From Paris down to Turkey' goes the third line of the Allez Allez Allez battlecry sung by those who went and those who weren't even born. Liverpool fans are a sentimental bunch and talk of Istanbul can't help but conjure up the opening bars of the Beatles song In My Life. Not just the stuff of legend, it's been the stuff of stage shows, plays, books, documentaries and movies.

Arguably it helps that it happened when it did – in an age, relatively speaking, of technological innocence. Phones in 2005 weren't nearly as smart as they are today. People sent old-fashioned text messages and still used cameras to take photos. Selfies? Behave. There was no Twitter, Instagram, WhatsApp or Tik-Tok, no apps to book flights and hotels, no Google Maps to guide you wherever you wanted to go, and YouTube had only just been launched.

VAR? Don't even go there.

Much has changed in the real world over the last two decades. Anfield has two magnificent new stands which have increased the ground's capacity from 45,000 or so to over 60,000. (Why, while we're here, isn't there a mural somewhere on the streets of L4 for Istanbul?) From the highest rows of the Main Stand you can see the city skyline, transformed by developments like the LiverpoolONE shopping complex, which was a construction site back in 2005, and the boost of European Capital of Culture status in 2008.

The Ataturk, a mere three years old in 2005, has since welcomed the Reds back twice: for a Champions League group match against Galatasaray the following year and a Europa League round-of-32 second leg away to Besiktas in 2015, neither game going Liverpool's way. It also hosted the 2023 Champions League final between Manchester City and another team from Milan, the black-and-blues of Inter.

Back in town, the breathtaking Hagia Sophia now presides over the west bank of the Bosporus as a mosque again, having been a museum when Reds with weary heads marvelled at its minarets and mosaics the morning after the night before. Istanbul itself continues to grow and sprawl, its population rising by three million to 16 million over the last 20 years and its urban area now measuring nearly 1,000 square miles.

This writer, like so many fans, has his little stash of 2005 memorabilia: travel documents and boarding passes from the earlier round-by-round trips to Leverkusen, Turin and West London; a set of 12 unused postcards of Istanbul and some grainy Taksim Square photos taken on a disposable camera; an official DVD of the final which to this day remains unwatched; a copy of

the Liverpool Daily Post newspaper from Thursday 26 May with the banner header 'KINGS OF EUROPE' (the paper was closed down in 2013 after 158 years of publication) and a copy of the Observer Sport section from Sunday 29 May.

The latter's front page carries an image from an international friendly between the USA and England in Chicago which Sven-Goran Eriksson's side had won 2-1 thanks to a brace from young midfield debutant Kieran Richardson. Next to it is a column by the paper's chief sports writer, Kevin Mitchell, which concludes: "Of the many reflections on the 'miracle of Istanbul', as it will come to be known, the most eloquent came not from a professional writer but a player. 'I'm enjoying this triumph like a child', said Xabi Alonso, scorer of Liverpool's equaliser. If there is a secret to the magic, it might lie there. In our innocent past."

Last but not least among my personal memorabilia: a special-edition Lonely Planet city guidebook, inside which is a Turkish five-lira banknote and my own torn, creased and precious match ticket and stub. North Tribune Lower Level, Block 307, Row 14, Seat 362. Behind the goal and just to the left, where no one scored that night but the spot-kick drama unfolded. Price: €20.

Twenty Euros. Don't even go there either.

As for 20 years, that's just crazy. Of the other Champions League finals in the meantime, Athens in 2007 was a very different vibe – anyone who went will say the same thing. For a long-distance odyssey undertaken by so many intrepid supporters, Kyiv in 2018 has its own kind of magic – if only the final had been as much fun. Madrid in 2019 is beloved for the pre-match parties bathed in sunshine before the collective release

"Football never stops being astonishing. That's the best thing about it – its stubborn capacity for surprise. The more the technocrats programme it down to the smallest detail, the more the powerful manipulate it, football continues to be the art of the unforeseeable"

of tension when Divock Origi settled a tight all-English affair. The less said about Paris in 2022, the better.

Nothing comes close to Istanbul. Nothing ever will. It belongs not just to Liverpool – to the club and the fans and all those who played their part that night – it belongs to everyone who loves football. The Uruguayan writer Eduardo Galeano, author of Soccer in Sun and Shadow, was one of those and he may well have had Istanbul in mind when he wrote the following...

"Football never stops being astonishing. That's the best thing about it – its stubborn capacity for surprise. The more the technocrats programme it down to the smallest detail, the more the powerful manipulate it, football continues to be the art of the unforeseeable.

"When you least expect it, the impossible occurs."

ISTANBUL
IN POPULAR CULTURE

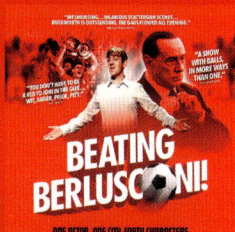

Beating Berlusconi: a one-man comedy show starring Paul Duckworth which tells the true story of Liverpool fan Mark Radley, who bluffed his way into the VIP suite of Silvio Berlusconi, the Italian prime minister and media tycoon, during the 2005 final. It debuted in 2015 and is returning for two more performances in Liverpool to celebrate the 20th anniversary of Istanbul.

One Night in Istanbul: a hit play about two Scouse cabbies who take their sons to the final with hilarious consequences, it was written by Reds fan Nicky Allt. Its various runs have featured cameo appearances on stage by Rafa Benitez, Steven Gerrard, Jamie Carragher, Kenny Dalglish, John Aldridge, Phil Neal, David Fairclough and Sammy Lee, and it was adapted for the big screen in 2014.

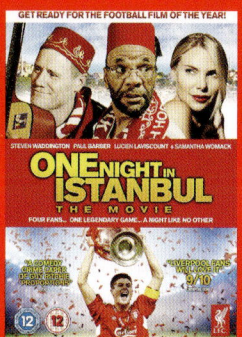

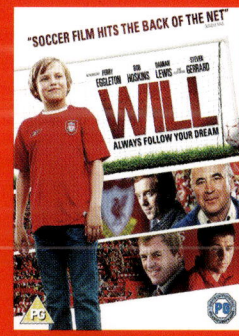

Will: 2011 movie starring real-life Liverpool supporter Damian Lewis as the father of an eleven-year-old boy who gives his son tickets for the final before unexpectedly dying. Alone, Will embarks on an epic journey to Istanbul. Steven Gerrard, Jamie Carragher and Kenny Dalglish all make brief appearances.

Fifteen Minutes that Shook the World: local-born actor Neil Fitzmaurice played Rafa in this short movie scripted by Dave Kirby. It starred Andrew Schofield as a TV journalist investigating what happened in the Reds dressing-room at half-time, alongside Didi Hamann, Steven Gerrard and Jamie Carragher.

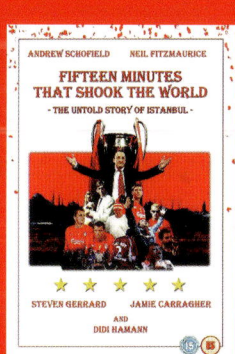

THE ROAD TO ISTANBUL

It was a long road to glory, starting in the qualifying rounds at the Arnold Schwarzenegger Stadium. Here and on the pages that follow is the story of how the Reds reached the 2004/05 UEFA Champions League final...

THIRD QUALIFYING ROUND, FIRST LEG

GRAZER AK 0
LIVERPOOL 2
Goals: Gerrard (23, 79)
10.08.04 • Attendance: 15,000

LIVERPOOL: Dudek; Josemi, Carragher, Hyypia, Riise; Finnan (Potter), Gerrard (Warnock), Hamann, Kewell; Baros (Diao), Cisse.

Liverpool's first competitive match under the management of Rafael Benitez ended in a comfortable 2-0 win at the Arnold Schwarzenegger Stadium.

Skipper Steven Gerrard was the destroyer with a long-range effort before the break and a predator-like strike before the end. Gerrard also got a raw deal when he had another spectacular effort disallowed - depriving him of a hat-trick.

Michael Owen was named among Liverpool's substitutes pending his move to Real Madrid but Liverpool were never going to risk an injury to the striker, particularly as they didn't want Los Blancos to haggle over the fee if Owen was ineligible for Europe. Owen duly said his farewells after 13 years at Liverpool with new striker Djibril Cisse, whose move had been agreed by Benitez's predecessor Gerard Houllier, making his debut. The Reds new-look strike partnership of Cisse and Milan Baros made an encouraging start in Austria.

Benitez introduced his Kindergarten Kop with Stephen Warnock and Darren Potter handed Liverpool debuts as substitutes and by the end it looked like had been well and truly terminated although there was to be a twist at Anfield.

THIRD QUALIFYING ROUND, SECOND LEG

LIVERPOOL 0
GRAZER AK 1
Goals: Tokic (55)
24.08.04 • Attendance: 42,950

LIVERPOOL: Dudek; Henchoz, Carragher, Hyypia, Riise; Diao, Potter, Gerrard, Kewell (Warnock); Baros (Hamann), Cisse (Sinama-Pongolle).

Grazer recorded a shock win at Anfield but it wasn't enough to stop Rafa's Reds from progressing to the Champions League group stage. Liverpool were poor on the night and a powerful 55th minute strike from Mario Tokic made for an uncomfortable final half-hour for Kopites.

The Reds created little and didn't deserve to win although they should have been up against 10 men when René Aluhauser was booked twice but the referee failed to send him off.

Sub Florent Sinama-Pongolle was denied by goalkeeper Andreas Schranz with a rare Liverpool attempt on goal, while the Reds only just avoided extra-time with Jerzy Dudek parrying a header from forward Roland Kollman and Tokic seeing another attempt whistle just wide of the target.

On this evidence there was little to suggest that Liverpool would be a real threat in the tournament proper.

GROUP STAGE, MATCHDAY ONE

LIVERPOOL 2
AS MONACO 0

Goals: Cisse (22), Baros (84)
15.09.04 • Attendance: 33,517

LIVERPOOL: Dudek; Josemi, Carragher, Hyypia, Riise; Finnan, Gerrard, Alonso, Kewell (Warnock); Garcia (Biscan), Cisse (Baros).

Djibril Cisse slammed home his first goal at Anfield as Liverpool got their group stage campaign off to a flying start against the previous season's beaten finalists. The French international striker fired home before the break after a neat passing move between Luis Garcia and Steven Gerrard as the Reds dominated the game.

Cisse should have scored a second after the break but it was substitute Milan Baros who finished Monaco off with an individual effort six minutes from time. He took a pass from Josemi, cut inside and then clipped his shot over Monaco keeper Flavio Roma.

The visitors produced only one attempt of real note but Jerzy Dudek was alert to keep out Emmanuel Adebayor's header from Mohamed Kallon's corner. Liverpool fans left the stadium in a far more confident manner than they had a few weeks earlier after the Reds had been beaten at home by Grazer in the second leg of the qualifier at Anfield.

GROUP STAGE, MATCHDAY TWO

OLYMPIAKOS 1
LIVERPOOL 0

Goals: Stoltidis (17)
28.09.04 • Attendance: 33,000

LIVERPOOL: Dudek; Josemi (Cisse), Carragher, Hyypia, Riise; Finnan, Hamann (Diao), Alonso, Warnock (Kewell); Garcia, Baros.

Liverpool turned in a particularly poor display in Greece and were lucky to get away with a one goal defeat.

Ieroklis Stoltidis headed home the winner from Rivaldo's free-kick in the first half following a foul by Stephen Warnock on the edge of the area and Olympiakos were unfortunate not to add further to their tally despite having Anastasos Pantos dismissed.

Olympiakos demonstrated the strength of the competition by dominating possession for long periods as the Reds struggled to string many passes together on a collective off-night. Giovanni and Pantelis Kafes went close with headers while Liverpool's best, and almost only, opportunity came when Baros played Harry Kewell through on goal only for the linesman to flag for offside.

It was the first time Liverpool had lost to Greek opposition but they could have few complaints as they left the Yorgos Karaiskakis Stadium.

LIVERPOOL 0
DEPORTIVO LA CORUNA 0
19.10.04 • Attendance: 40,236

LIVERPOOL: Kirkland; Josemi, Carragher, Hyypia, Traore; Garcia (Sinama-Pongolle), Hamann, Alonso, Riise (Kewell), Baros, Cisse (Finnan).

It was to be an evening of frustration at Anfield as Liverpool threw everything but the kitchen sink at Deportivo but just couldn't break down their resolute defence

The Spaniards arrived at Anfield intent on keeping a clean sheet and as a result it was Liverpool who made all the running. The Reds, missing Steven Gerrard through injury, were sent out to attack although they survived an early scare when John Arne Riise was forced to clear Cesar Martin's header off the line.

Djibril Cisse, Milan Baros and Luis Garcia should all have scored before the break.

Cisse was denied in the 18th minute by Manuel Pablo and when Baros rounded keeper Jose Molina nine minutes later he seemed certain to score until Pablo appeared from nowhere to make another goal-saving tackle. Garcia was then denied by an extraordinary save from Molina. Xabi Alonso's shot had deflected into Garcia's path and he smashed a first-time effort goalwards only to see the Depor keeper instinctively thrust his arms upwards and somehow deflect the ball over the bar.

Chances were at a premium in the second-half and substitute Harry Kewell came closest to breaking the deadlock when his 91st minute free-kick flashed just wide of Molina's goal but it simply wasn't to be Liverpool's night.

DEPORTIVO LA CORUNA 0
LIVERPOOL 1
Goals: Andrade (OG) (14)
03.11.04 • Attendance: 32,000

LIVERPOOL: Kirkland; Josemi, Carragher, Hyypia, Traore; Garcia (Alonso), Hamann, Biscan, Riise, Baros (Sinama-Pongolle), Kewell (Finnan).

Igor Biscan was the unlikely star of the show as Liverpool recorded a vital 1-0 win at The Riazor on Rafael Benitez's return to Spain.

With Xabi Alonso struggling with a calf injury and Steven Gerrard nursing a broken metatarsal, midfield responsibility was handed to Biscan and Didi Hamann. It took Biscan less than a minute to show he meant business when he played Milan Baros clean through but the Czech failed to go around keeper Jose Molina and the opportunity was wasted.

The Croatian was in top form and in the 14th minute was the architect of Liverpool's winner. Picking up the ball in the centre of midfield, Biscan made a clever feint to avoid one challenge before going on a driving run forward and spreading the ball out wide to John Arne Riise. The Norwegian crossed towards Baros but defender Jorge Andrade got to the ball first and could only look in horror as he sent it past Molina and into his own net. Riise almost doubled the lead before the break but Andrade cleared off the line.

With Josemi and Djimi Traore outstanding at full-back, Depor's dangerous wide men had little influence on the game.

The victory left Liverpool joint top of Group A.

AS MONACO 1
LIVERPOOL 0
Goals: Saviola (54)
23.11.04 • Attendance: 15,000

LIVERPOOL: Kirkland; Traore (Kewell), Carragher, Hyypia, Riise; Finnan, Hamann, Gerrard, Biscan, Garcia (Josemi (Warnock)), Mellor.

Nothing went Liverpool's way as they lost Luis Garcia, Josemi and Djimi Traore through injury before seeing Javier Saviola score a winner after controlling the ball with his hand.

Liverpool felt they were deserving of a point in the casino capital of Europe and but for the astonishing decision by Danish referee, Bo Larsen, they would have had one.

The Reds, clearly aggrieved, never really regained their composure and even Monaco coach Didier Deschamps admitted his side had been fortunate in his post-match analysis.

Youngster Neil Mellor, left to plough a lone furrow in attack without much in the way of support, had a goal disallowed as Liverpool's luck ran out on the night.

The latest injuries also meant Benitez's squad would be stretched to its limit ahead of the crucial clash with Olympiakos a couple of weeks later when the Reds would need to win their final group game in order to progress.

GROUP STAGE, MATCHDAY SIX

LIVERPOOL 3
OLYMPIAKOS 1

Goals: Sinama-Pongolle (47), Mellor (81),
Gerrard (86); Rivaldo (26)

08.12.04 • Attendance: 42,045

LIVERPOOL: Kirkland; Finnan (Josemi), Carragher, Hyypia, Traore (Sinama-Pongolle);
Nunez, Gerrard, Alonso, Riise; Kewell, Baros (Mellor).

On one of Anfield's greatest European nights, Liverpool booked their place in the last 16 of the Champions League with a heroic second-half display.

Rivaldo's first half free-kick looked to have ended the Reds' interest in the competition, but inspired performances from second half substitutes Florent Sinama-Pongolle and Neil Mellor turned the game on its head before Steven Gerrard smashed home a glorious late winner that will forever remain part of Anfield folklore.

It was mathematics rather than tactics that Kopites had on their minds when they arrived at the ground before kick-off. A 1-0 win would be enough to send Liverpool through but if Olympiakos scored the Reds needed to win by two clear goals, although they could sneak through with a 2-1 victory if Monaco lost in A Coruña. Anything other than a win and Liverpool were definitely out.

Benitez had selection problems. In addition to long-term casualties Djibril Cisse and Vladimir Smicer, Didi Hamann was suspended. Luis Garcia was ruled out with the hamstring he pulled in Monaco and Igor Biscan wasn't allowed to play because he'd suffered concussion a week earlier in a League Cup tie at Spurs.

It meant that Antonio Nunez was handed his first Champions League start on the right with Harry Kewell playing in the hole behind Milan Baros, himself back after missing the previous five games with a hamstring injury.

With a highly-charged Anfield backing them all the way, Liverpool started like a house on fire and forced three corners in the opening minute, the third of which Baros headed goalwards only to see the ball cleared off the line.

Sami Hyypia headed a good chance wide and Gerrard struck a post, but in the 27th minute Rivaldo won himself a free-kick on the edge of the box and curled it past Chris Kirkland. The Greeks went in at half-time a goal up and with the news from Spain that Monaco were several goals to the good, Benitez knew that his team had to score three times if they were to progress.

He responded by replacing Djimi Traore with Sinama-Pongolle at the interval and the change paid dividends straight away. Two minutes into the second half and Kewell got to the by-line and crossed for Sinama-Pongolle to score from close range. Liverpool were back in it.

Gerrard saw a brilliant long-range strike in the 62nd minute disallowed after Spanish referee Manuel Gonzalez adjudged Baros to have committed an offence earlier in the move.

With the clock ticking down, Benitez made his last throw of the dice, replacing the tiring Baros with Neil Mellor. Three minutes later Mellor poached a goal in typical fashion, tapping home after Nunez's header was saved by Antonios Nikopolidis. Now the Kop were trying to suck the ball into the net and, with just four minutes left, came a moment of sheer exhilaration.

Jamie Carragher played a high ball forward that Mellor brilliantly steered into the path of Gerrard who let it bounce once before striking a thunderbolt from just outside the box that flew past the Greek international keeper and into the net. Anfield erupted. The Olympiakos players looked stunned and had no answer. Against all odds, Liverpool were through to the last 16.

16

'I STILL GET
GOOSEBUMPS
THINKING ABOUT IT'

Former Reds striker and LFCTV pundit Neil Mellor relives one night against Olympiakos that changed the course of LFC history

On 8 December 2004, something happened at Anfield that changed the course of history.

Although Liverpool were beating Olympiakos by two goals to one in Liverpool in their final Champions League group match, the margin was not enough – the Greek champions would feature in the next round unless Liverpool scored again to seal progression at their opponent's expense.

Twenty-two-year-old Neil Mellor had been introduced as a substitute for Milan Baros with 12 minutes remaining with the game locked at one-all. Within 90 seconds he scrambled Liverpool into a lead, offering hope that the impossible could be achieved.

"I remember running up and down the touchline really fast trying to indicate to the manager that I was ready to come on for the whole of the second half," Mellor says.

"I was desperate for it. To be honest, I was disappointed not to get the call at half-time because Rivaldo's free-kick knocked the stuffing out of us. We needed a miracle."

Ten days before, Neil had scored the winner against Arsenal with a volley from 30 yards, which nestled in the bottom corner of Jens Lehmann's net right in front of the Kop. This was Arsenal's 'Invincibles' of the previous season, whose 49-game unbeaten run had only ended a month earlier with a controversial defeat at Manchester United.

"Our result against Arsenal gave us a belief that maybe wasn't there beforehand," Mellor recalls. "The performances in the league had been indifferent and we were finding it difficult to find a consistency in our game. But when you beat a team as good as Arsenal were around that time, especially in the final minute, you start to believe that you can beat anybody.

"The game is never over and we carried that attitude throughout the rest of the season."

That day, Mellor's strike was so late that he'd already asked Sol Campbell if he could swap shirts at the end. "Weirdly, Campbell saying yes gave me a little boost," he says.

"When the ball fell to me I didn't realise how far out I was. Lehmann's positioning was a bit off and I realised there was a gap. Luckily I caught it sweet but just as the ball left my foot [Patrick] Vieira gave me an elbow to the cheek. In normal circumstances I'd have gone down but within a split-second I realised I'd scored.

"After that, everything is a blur. During the match you don't usually hear the roar of the crowd because you're so focused. Even among the chaos of the celebrations though I managed to take it all in. I took more pleasure in seeing the fans go absolutely nuts than anything else. People were climbing over one another, losing themselves.

"It was a Sunday night and a couple of the boys were asking me to go to The Living Room [bar] in town to unwind. But I was so tired I went home and watched Match of the Day 2 with my mum and dad.

"Gordon Strachan was on there as a pundit being really positive about the way I'd played so I was made-up."

In between beating Arsenal and meeting Olympiakos, he started in Liverpool's League Cup victory at Tottenham Hotspur on penalties and a 1-1 draw at Aston Villa.

"As the Olympiakos game approached I was hopeful I'd get selected but wasn't absolutely convinced. Rafa [Benitez] proved throughout the season that he was prepared to throw a few surprises in his team selection. But I have to be honest and admit I wasn't surprised when I was named on the bench."

Mellor recalls the despondency in the dressing-room at half-time. Rivaldo's 26th minute free-kick had crept through a broken defensive wall, leaving goalkeeper Chris Kirkland motionless. "I couldn't see us winning from that point."

Suddenly, Jamie Carragher stood up.

"He was having none of it. Carra went around telling everybody we could still get through. The score in the other game [Monaco were beating Deportivo La Coruna 3-0] meant that we still had a chance but we needed a two-goal cushion to do it. In Istanbul maybe tactics helped turn it round – along with Stevie's massive

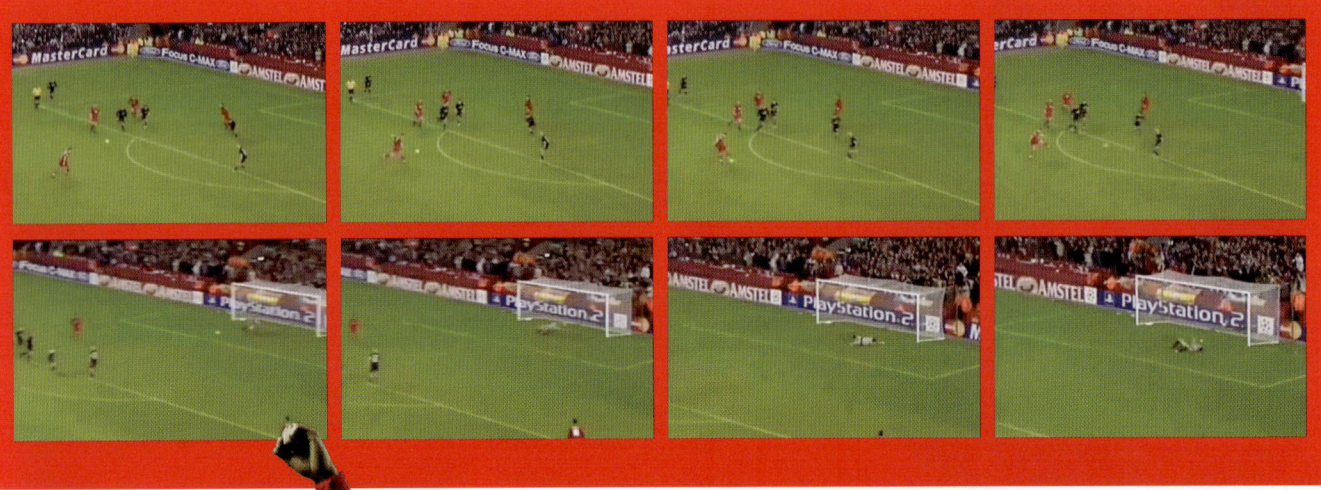

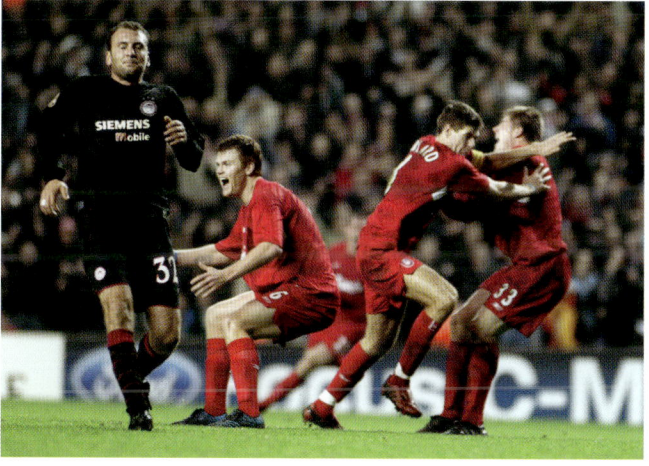

contribution obviously – but on this occasion it was purely Carra. We just needed to believe a bit more. He kept saying that if we got the next goal, Olympiakos might freeze and panic. He'd seen it happen to teams before, and he was right."

After Florent Sinama-Pongolle levelled the scores a few minutes into the second half, there was a long wait until Mellor's first contribution. "Stevie had a goal disallowed when the keeper spilled it and Harry Kewell had a glorious chance with a header. Then Xabi Alonso had a free-kick and I thought Carra was fouled and we should've had a penalty.

"But the ball kept pinging about the box. Eventually [Antonio] Nunez had another header saved and I reacted first with my toe-end to make it 2-1. I was buzzing but there was still work to be done."

Again Carragher appeared in a forward position, this time on the left. His cross towards the outside of the box was met by Mellor who cushioned it into the path of the waiting steam train that was Liverpool's captain.

"As soon as I saw Stevie running onto it, I knew he was going to score.

"He might have been 20 or 25 yards out but I'd seen him strike the ball a million times in training. There was no better midfielder in the country at doing that. Before I knew it, Stevie was past me celebrating in the Kop. I still get goosebumps thinking about that."

Unfortunately for Neil, it was the last time he would play in Liverpool's remarkable run to the final where AC Milan were leading 3-0 at half-time and somehow beaten.

"It was the best few weeks of my career. It frustrates me that injuries stopped me playing in more games for Liverpool, but at least I experienced moments that made a lot of people happy.

"For nights like that to happen, your best players have to step forward and use the emotion of the crowd as a strength.

"Many foreign players haven't experienced Anfield before. It does have an atmosphere that can make all the difference."

LAST 16, FIRST LEG

LIVERPOOL 3
BAYER LEVERKUSEN 1
Goals: Garcia (15), Riise (35), Hamann (90); Franca (90)
22.02.05 • Attendance: 40,942

LIVERPOOL: Dudek; Finnan, Carragher, Hyypia, Traore; Garcia, Biscan, Hamann, Riise (Smicer); Kewell (Le Tallec), Baros (Potter).

With Steven Gerrard suspended, it was Igor Biscan who stepped into his shoes and the Anfield cult figure was in inspirational form again. Right from the start of the game the pace of Liverpool's passing and movement unsettled their visitors and the in-form Germans were on the back foot.

Luis Garcia opened the scoring after Biscan stormed through the Leverkusen midfield and played an inch-perfect pass for the Spaniard to run onto and slip under the body of keeper Jorg Butt.

The German side responded by looking for an away goal and striker Dimitar Berbatov, who had scored one of the goals that helped to eliminate Liverpool from the 2002 Champions League quarter-final between the sides, should have equalised in the 29th minute. Steve Finnan's attempted back header hit Sami Hyypia and the Bulgarian raced clean through but rolled the ball wide of Jerzy Dudek's post.

He was punished moments later when John Arne Riise smashed home a powerful free-kick that beat Butt at his near post. Didi Hamann appeared to have ended it in the 90th minute with another free-kick.

However, an injury-time fumble by Dudek allowed Franca to steal a precious away goal to silence Anfield and give the Germans renewed hope of repeating their success against the Reds of three years earlier.

BAYER LEVERKUSEN 1
LIVERPOOL 3

Goals: Garcia (28, 32), Baros (67); Krzynowek (88)
09.03.05 • Attendance: 23,000

LIVERPOOL: Dudek; Finnan (Nunez), Carragher (Welsh), Hyypia, Warnock; Gerrard, Biscan, Hamann (Smicer), Riise; Garcia, Baros.

All the talk before the game had been about Leverkusen's exceptional European form at the BayArena, but Liverpool turned in an accomplished display in Germany. After a minute's silence in honour of the late great Rinus Michels, Liverpool were in control of the game from the start and Luis Garcia killed the tie off with a double strike in the space of four minutes.

The diminutive Spaniard cancelled out Leverkusen's away goal in the 28th minute when he headed home Steven Gerrard's pinpoint cross from the right. He then finished the home side off completely when Igor Biscan powerfully headed a Gerrard corner goalwards and Garcia cleverly touched the ball past the diving Jorg Butt from close range.

Liverpool were in cruise control after that and Milan Baros added a third after good work from Gerrard again.

Rafael Benitez then had the luxury of resting players and ended up fielding an unlikely back four of Antonio Nunez, Sami Hyypia, Igor Biscan and Stephen Warnock with a late consolation from Jacek Kryznowek in no way taking the gloss off the night for the men in yellow.

QUARTER FINAL, FIRST LEG

LIVERPOOL 2
JUVENTUS 1
Goals: Hyypia (10), Garcia (25); Cannavaro (63)
05.04.05 • Attendance: 41,216

LIVERPOOL: Carson; Finnan, Carragher, Hyypia, Traore; Garcia, Biscan, Gerrard, Riise; Le Tallec (Smicer), Baros (Nunez).

Twenty years after the horror of Heysel, Liverpool and Juventus met again. Inevitably the events of the 1985 European Cup final, at which 39 people lost their lives, dominated the headlines. Before kick-off the message was 'memoria e amicizia' - in memory and friendship. The Kop held up a mosaic that simply said 'amicizia', while Ian Rush, Phil Neal and Michel Platini presented a specially-crafted plaque to the travelling Juve fans.

On the pitch Rafael Benitez had sprung a surprise by starting youngsters Scott Carson and Anthony Le Tallec. With the noise levels high, Liverpool attacked from the start and within 10 seconds of Juventus kicking off, Milan Baros had a shot that was deflected wide for a corner. Juve had only conceded two Champions League goals all season, but it took Sami Hyypia just 10 minutes to get his name on the scoresheet when he cracked home a wonderful left-footed volley after Luis Garcia flicked Steven Gerrard's corner on. Garcia then added a stunning second 15 minutes later with a left-footed half volley from 30-yards out that dipped over the stranded Gianluigi Buffon.

Zlatan Ibrahimovic hit a post and Carson saved from Alessandro Del Piero as Juve pushed for an away goal and they got one in the second half when Fabio Cannavaro's header squirmed past Carson to leave Liverpool facing a tricky trip to Turin.

QUARTER FINAL, SECOND LEG

JUVENTUS 0
LIVERPOOL 0

13.04.05 • Attendance: 59,400

LIVERPOOL: Dudek; Finnan, Carragher, Hyypia, Traore; Nunez (Smicer), Alonso, Biscan, Riise; Garcia (Le Tallec), Baros (Cisse).

As expected, Liverpool received a hostile reception in Turin with many Juventus fans taking the opportunity to make their feelings known about Brussels in 1985.

Rafael Benitez's Reds needed a draw to progress, but with Steven Gerrard and Didi Hamann both ruled out through injury, the task was made more difficult. Igor Biscan stepped in again and Xabi Alonso returned to play his first game since breaking an ankle against Chelsea on New Year's Day.

Five of the Liverpool team that started in Turin had also started in the ignominious FA Cup defeat at Burnley just three months earlier. They more than made up for that in Italy with a display of defiance and courage to secure a 0-0 draw that was likened to Liverpool's 1-1 result at Bayern Munich in 1981.

Juventus, who would later go on to win Serie A, were limited to just two clear-cut chances all night. Zlatan Ibrahimovic headed over in the first half and after the break Jerzy Dudek managed to claw the ball off the line after Fabio Cannavaro's had hit the post and deflected goalwards off Djimi Traore.

At the other end, Milan Baros missed a gilt-edged chance when he forced his way through only to shoot wide. The sight of the night, though, was Djibril Cisse's substitute appearance just six months after he had suffered a horrific double leg fracture at Blackburn which almost left him needing an amputation.

It was an evening and a return that the word 'heroic' was invented for.

SEMI-FINAL, FIRST LEG

CHELSEA 0
LIVERPOOL 0

27.04.05 • Attendance: 40,497

LIVERPOOL: Dudek; Finnan, Carragher, Hyypia, Traore; Garcia (Smicer), Biscan (Kewell), Alonso, Riise; Gerrard, Baros (Cisse).

Unbeaten at Stamford Bridge under Jose Mourinho and having scored four goals apiece in their previous two Champions League home games against Barcelona and Bayern Munich, Chelsea looked like being formidable semi-final opponents.

They'd already beaten Liverpool three times – including in the Carling Cup final in Cardiff – although they had been incredibly lucky to win two of those games.

With Didi Hamann still out injured, Igor Biscan sat alongside Xabi Alonso in front of the back four while Steven Gerrard – who was playing despite having an operation to remove an abscess from his mouth on the morning of the game – asked to play behind Milan Baros. The system worked well and Chelsea only created two clear chances of note in the whole game with Didier Drogba firing wide and Frank Lampard blasting over.

Baros was unlucky not to give Liverpool the lead and the vital away goal, when he headed Gerrard's cross goalwards only for Petr Cech to somehow claw it away. Chelsea got more anxious as the second half went on, but with Jamie Carragher in imperious form at the heart of defence and Sami Hyypia, Djimi Traore and Steve Finnan all excelling, Jerzy Dudek didn't have a single save to make all night and the game finished goalless.

Not even Mourinho's post-match confidence could dissuade Kopites now that Liverpool were on the verge of something special.

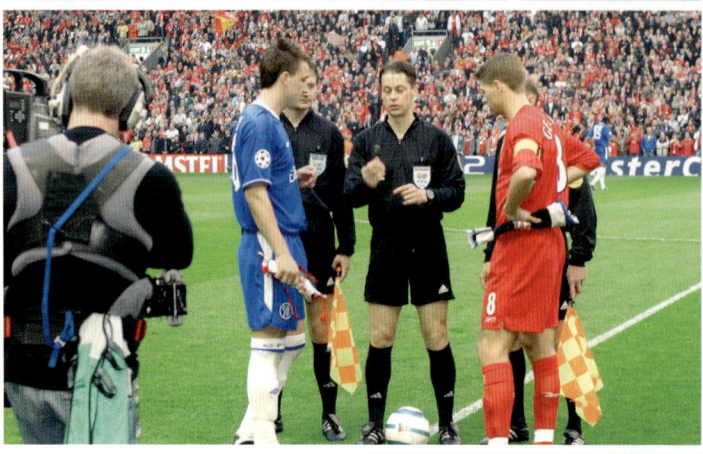

L.F.C.

LIVERPOOL 1
CHELSEA 0
Goal: Garcia (4)
03.05.05 • Attendance: 42,529

LIVERPOOL: Dudek; Finnan, Carragher, Hyypia, Traore; Gerrard (Smicer), Biscan, Hamann, Riise; Garcia (Nunez), Baros (Cisse).

After winning the Premier League title just three days earlier and having scored in every away European game they had played for the last two seasons, Chelsea arrived on Merseyside full of confidence.

They didn't just come up against Liverpool though – they faced arguably the most partisan, awesome atmosphere that Anfield has ever produced. At times the noise was spine-tingling as the sight of thousands of scarves being swirled around heads all around the ground inspired the players. Within four minutes, Liverpool – who were missing the suspended Xabi Alonso – were ahead.

Milan Baros latched on to Steven Gerrard's incisive through ball and was brought down by Petr Cech as he chipped the ball over him but, as the Liverpool fans screamed for a penalty, Luis Garcia flicked the ball goalwards and, although William Gallas cleared it, the Slovakian linesman adjudged it to have crossed the line. One-nil Liverpool.

Chelsea now had to attack but couldn't find a way through a resilient Liverpool defence which was superbly marshalled by the outstanding Jamie Carragher with Didi Hamann, who had just returned from injury, protecting his back four superbly.

Chelsea's best chance fell to Eidur Gudjohnsen deep into the six minutes of injury-time that were added on, but he fired wide and moments later the celebrations began. They continued all the way to Istanbul where Liverpool would take on AC Milan in their sixth European Cup final.

"I am sure it was a GOAL.

I'm sure it crossed the line because I was standing only four yards away from it"

Semi-final hero LUIS GARCIA on his 'ghost goal' against Chelsea, his stunner against Juventus in the quarter-final and reflections on his debut season at Anfield

It has split debate among Liverpool and Chelsea supporters for the two decades since but Luis Garcia is in no doubt that his early strike in front of the Kop was valid.

Chelsea fans were feeling blue after the match officials ruled Garcia's effort had crossed the line moments after goalkeeper Petr Cech had wiped out Milan Baros.

On the anniversary of the goal or at Hallowe'en, Garcia sometimes takes to social media wearing a white cloak to reference the 'ghost' goal!

"I suppose for the club the goal I scored against Chelsea was maybe the best because this club had waited such a long time to get back into the final of the UEFA Champions League," he recalled. "It was not the best goal of my career but it was the goal that took us over the finishing line so I am very happy with it.

"I am sure it was a goal. I'm sure it crossed the line because I was standing only four yards away from it. I waited until the ball crossed before I started to celebrate so in my mind I am sure there was no doubt. The only person who had a view like mine was the linesman and he also gave the goal to us.

"It was a very different kind of goal for me. It was a striker's goal, a goal poacher's goal and it was nice to score one like that. You don't always have to score pretty goals in this game to win things. For me it is not about how the ball makes it into the net, just knowing it is there is enough."

How the ball entered the net against Juventus in the last eight clash at Anfield was, however, a thing of beauty - a glorious dipping volley from 25-yards after taking Anthony Le Tallec's pass in his stride.

"My favourite goal of that season was the one against Juventus," he reflects. "It was a very nice goal to score for me and it was special because it was an important goal in an important game. It was one of the best, one of the most beautiful I got in my career."

Soon after arriving at Anfield from Barcelona in the summer of 2004, Garcia had a vision of Liverpool playing in the Champions League final and it almost manifested itself.

"I said that season that I had had a dream about winning the final of the UEFA Champions League and I was lucky because we all worked hard - the players and the fans - to make sure it came true.

"I say the fans too because they must have had no voice left against Chelsea and they must have been tired at the end of the game, almost as tired as we were. I'm not sure if we would have made it without them."

Although Garcia scored in every knockout round of the competition leading up to the final, he admits he often felt he could have done better in that first season on Merseyside.

"I knew I could do more things and have a bigger influence on

games. I played a lot of games and scored some goals but I would like to have been a lot more involved in the games.

"When I played my first games of the season I was surprised by the physical side of the English game. Everyone was always battling and fighting for every loose ball and I felt I had maybe made a mistake coming here because I was losing out a lot of times. But with the support of my team-mates and the people on the street I adapted my game.

"Some people told me in the summer that I was making a big mistake coming to Liverpool. They told me that I would get

chances at Barcelona and that they were building something very special at the Nou Camp and I would be wrong to move on at that time.

"But when I made my decision, and I decided I wanted to come to Liverpool I felt only happiness and joy. I felt positive I was making the correct decision for me, my career and for my family.

"I moved to a club with a great manager, with great players who were also building something very special and I ended that season by winning the Champions League."

FLYING THE RED FLAG

Channeling the spirit of 1977 and a famous Joey Jones banner, the official LFC Weekly Magazine produced their own flag for Jamie Carragher in the build-up to the final. *Here's how they told the story...*

Liverpool players are hoping to write another chapter in Liverpool's glorious European history in Istanbul.

Meanwhile, the fans have been busy writing slogans for banners to show their support for the Redmen. And LFC magazine has been joining in.

Kopites have always been one step ahead when it comes to banner - writing, with the 'Joey Jones ate the frog's legs' banner from the European Cup final in Rome 1977, the most famous of them all.

We decided to come up with something that would capture the same mood for Istanbul 2005, so we created this special 10-foot wide banner in honour of the European Cup heroics of Jamie Carragher this campaign.

We showed it to Carra, appointed captain for the day for the send-off against Aston Villa at Anfield, and he was made up.

As he was posing for pictures with it he told us: "The main thing is winning that European Cup and bringing it home, but it would be great if the banner went down in history a bit like the Joey Jones one."

The banner was well-received as it was shown on the Kop for the first time as it set out on its journey to Istanbul.

HOW WE MADE IT...

1 First we bought a giant sheet of red material (10ft by 6ft) and a similar sized sheet of white fabric for a total of £20 from Abakhan Fabrics in Stafford Street, Liverpool.

2 We created templates for the individual letters we needed and worked out how many of each we would need to cut-out. eg: ten E's, three W's and eight N's.

3 Using a pencil we traced round the letters and cut them out using scissors.

4 We placed the red fabric flat out on the floor and began to spell the words out and space the letters until we were happy with the positioning.

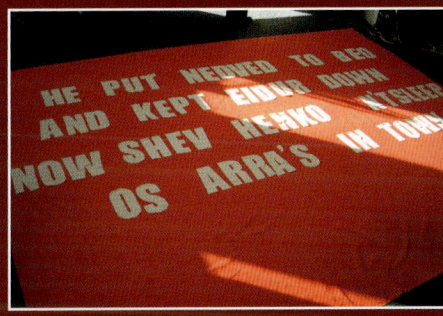

5 Finally, we applied some fabric glue and left it to dry overnight.

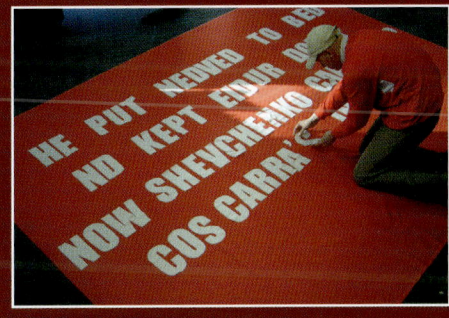

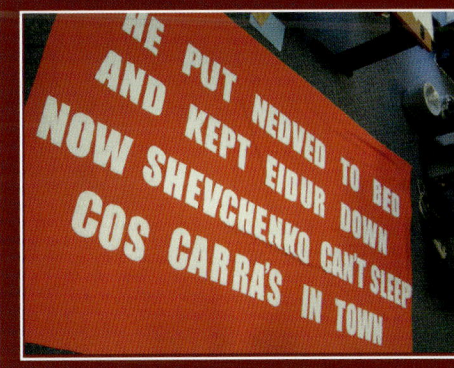

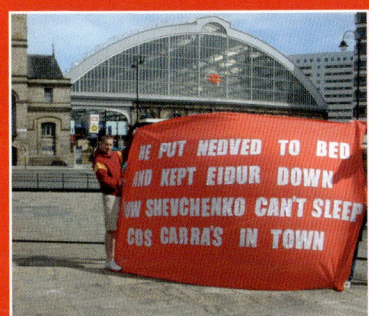

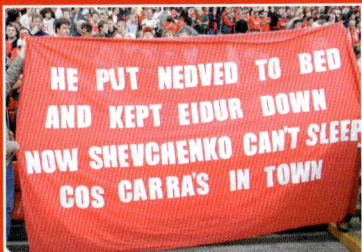

The city of memories and hopes was how Istanbul's marketeers saw fit to describe this sprawling metropolis in the run-up to the UEFA Champions League final.

They surely could not have realised how fitting that description would become because after 120 minutes of breathtaking action and the other 10 agonising minutes required to complete the penalty shoot-out in the Ataturk Stadium, the greatest hopes of every Liverpool supporter were realised and a quite amazing comeback was etched in the memory for all time.

This venerable competition has seen some epic encounters in its long and illustrious history but never before has a comeback been staged so magnificently as that which Rafa's Reds effected in the second 45 minutes in Turkey. Lazarus himself would have been proud of the recovery.

Three-nil down inside just 44 minutes, few gave Liverpool even the faintest glimmer of hope for the second half. Much of the talk on the press benches during a disbelieving interval concerned damage limitation. Indeed some of those Liverpool supporters who had travelled to Turkey decided at half-time that all was lost and the best thing they could do was simply head for the exits and disappear into the night. More fool them.

The more determined amongst the 40,000 Kopites simply sang 'we're gonna win 4-3'.

At the time it felt like bluster, or more likely gallows humour but they were not a million miles away from the correct result.

AC MILAN 3
LIVERPOOL 3

Goals: Maldini (1), Crespo (39, 44); Gerrard (54), Smicer (56), Alonso (60)

25.05.05 • Attendance: 69,000
Referee: Manuel Gonzalez (Spain)

Liverpool won 3-2 on penalties

Penalties: Serginho (0-0), Hamann (0-1); Pirlo (0-1) Cisse (0-2); Tomasson (1-2), Riise (1-2); Kaka (2-2), Smicer (2-3); Shevchenko (2-3).

LIVERPOOL: (4-1-4-1) Dudek; Finnan (Hamann), Carragher, Hyypia, Traore; Garcia, Gerrard, Alonso, Riise; Kewell (Smicer); Baros (Cisse). Subs not used: Carson, Josemi, Nunez, Biscan.

AC MILAN: (4-3-1-2) Dida; Cafu, Stam, Nesta, Maldini; Gattuso (Rui Costa), Seedorf (Serginho), Pirlo; Kaka; Shevchenko, Crespo (Tomasson). Subs not used: Abbiati, Kaladze, Costacurta, Dhorasoo.

Admittedly, the first half was as wretched a performance as the side had produced under the year-long stewardship of Rafa Benitez.

All week Milan coach Carlo Ancelotti had promised an electric start from his side, the normally cautious Italian had even gone so far as to suggest that his side would break the deadlock inside the first two minutes.

He didn't even have to wait that long.

Milan's first attack was a rapid raid down Liverpool's left flank. The elegant, flowing Kaka ran at Djimi Traore - hoping to exploit the space behind the Frenchman. Even with John Arne Riise in attendance, Traore was deceived by the quick feet of the 23-year-old and could only haul his man to the deck. Andrea Pirlo took charge of the set piece and that fact alone should have struck fear into Liverpool hearts.

The Italian international was arguably the game's finest dead-ball specialist and although this one wasn't one of his best deliveries it was still good enough to find Paolo Maldini in space at the edge of the box. The Milan skipper's drive was struck down and into the lush green turf but spun up and beyond the helpless Jerzy Dudek for a crushing early blow delivered in only 52 seconds.

There were two more similarly discouraging moments in a first half of which the less said the better. On-loan Chelsea forward Hernan Crespo had menaced the Reds defence earlier in the game when he got his head on another Pirlo cross first but his net-bound header was cleared on the line by Luis Garcia. There was no such barrier soon after.

His first goal, and Milan's second, was the product of a flowing move involving Clarence Seedorf, Pirlo, Kaka and Andriy Shevchenko. The last of these delivered a cut-back so precise that the Argentinean could not have missed at the back post.

However, Liverpool were rightly aggrieved that this second goal was allowed to stand. Milan's breakaway came directly from a handball from Alessandro Nesta inside his own box.

Garcia feinted to shoot but cut inside his marker instead, and in an act of desperation Nesta threw his body in the way of the ball. Replays clearly showed, as did the naked eye, that the only part of his anatomy to make contact with the ball was his right elbow and it was not accidental.

It might have been had Nesta not got up protesting his innocence informing the referee that the ball had struck his head. He knew what the travelling Kop knew only too well - it was a penalty.

Perhaps the Italian journalists who turned up at Anfield for the pre-final media day knew exactly what they were doing when they

to influence the game. It turned out to be a tactical masterstroke from Benitez since Kaka disappeared completely from the game and as his influence faded, so Steven Gerrard's began to grow.

It was the skipper who gave Liverpool hope with a looping header. His last cranial involvement in a cup final allowed Chelsea back into the League Cup final in Cardiff. But this time he rose to meet Riise's cross at the right end and his header could not have been more in the top corner of Dida's net had he placed the ball there with his hands.

It was game on as a new sense of urgency descended from the terraces engulfing the players. Vladimir Smicer was given one last outing when Harry Kewell was forced from the field in the first half and the Czech was to play a significant role in what remained of the game.

There was no real danger when Vladi collected the ball 30-yards from goal. His touch took him five yards closer though and he unleashed a fierce drive that flew into the bottom corner of the goal.

It had taken only 45 minutes to seemingly extinguish Liverpool's dreams but they were thoroughly re-ignited in just six second-half minutes.

Jamie Carragher's angled through ball and flick from Luis Garcia put Gerrard in behind the Milan defence with a chance he looked destined to take when the ball sat up perfectly for a shot. Perfect that was before Reno Gattuso's clumsy challenge dumped him on the deck.

Goalscoring opportunities don't come any clearer but the referee chose to avoid a red card and didn't even book the former Rangers player.

That didn't bother Xabi Alonso who assumed responsibility from the spot and although he saw his effort saved by the athletic Dida, he was on hand to force home the rebound. It was as well those parts of the Ataturk Stadium housing the Reds fans were roofless, otherwise it may well have been blown from its fixings.

As three sides of the ground rejoiced, Milan looked shell-shocked and the Kopites' dream could be reality once more.

The remainder of normal time was cagey with neither side prepared to risk all for fear of a disaster at the other end. Extra-time was nerve-shredding but not because Milan were dominant.

That passed with the half-time interval but Liverpool stood on the precipice of the greatest comeback of any Champions League final and the burden weighed heavy. Two Dudek saves from Shevchenko - the second breathtaking in both its bravery and its timing - ensured penalties would be a deciding factor. Liverpool's bottle, guts, heart, fight - call it what you want - made sure it was decided in the Reds' favour.

Serginho was first from 12 yards but he blazed high, handing Liverpool the early superiority. That was confirmed when Didi Hamann scored. Pirlo was next for Milan but Dudek saved well, allowing Djibril Cisse to open up a two-goal Reds lead.

Jon Dahl Tomasson did likewise for Milan before Riise missed for Liverpool. In truth it owed more to the reflexes and reach of Dida who got down well to the low shot. Kaka levelled for Milan. Liverpool's next taker was Smicer who strode forward knowing this would be his last kick as a Liverpool player.

He was hero and not villain, rifling home into the corner. Shevchenko had to score, but then he always does, doesn't he? Not on this occasion as Dudek threw himself right to save and in doing so created history.

Wild celebrations ensued as players leapt the advertising boards to join the jubilant fans.

How they summoned up the energy is as much a mystery as what Rafa put into his half-time team talk to effect such a dramatic transformation in his players.

It was a crazy night, in a crazy place but the European Cup has come home to Anfield for keeps.

New York is known as the city that never sleeps. Yet Istanbul that Wednesday night was the city that wasn't allowed to sleep as the Reds' celebrations roared on into Thursday, and no doubt Friday and the Bank Holiday weekend too.

asked Liverpool's Spanish contingent if having a fellow countryman in charge of the final would aid the Reds' cause. Their line of questioning was widely reported, perhaps wide enough to reach the ears of the match referee who seemed determined to prove himself beyond reproach.

Sometimes he tried too hard to be fair, but more of that later.

If there was an air of injustice about Crespo's first goal Liverpool could have no complaints about his second and Milan's third. It was simply the finish of a man full of confidence since it takes a brave man to attempt such a delicate chip over the on-rushing Dudek in what was a vital game. His stabbed lob, if such a thing exists, was exquisite and half-time could not come quickly enough for the rocking Reds.

Benitez had made few mistakes in his Liverpool tenure but perhaps in the cold light of day he will review his team selection believing he gave the mercurial Kaka too much room in which to play for those 45 minutes. They do say though that mistakes are fine so long as you learn from them and the arrival of Didi Hamann at the interval ensured Kaka would have to work harder

ISTANBUL UNCUT

IAN TOPPING R.I.P

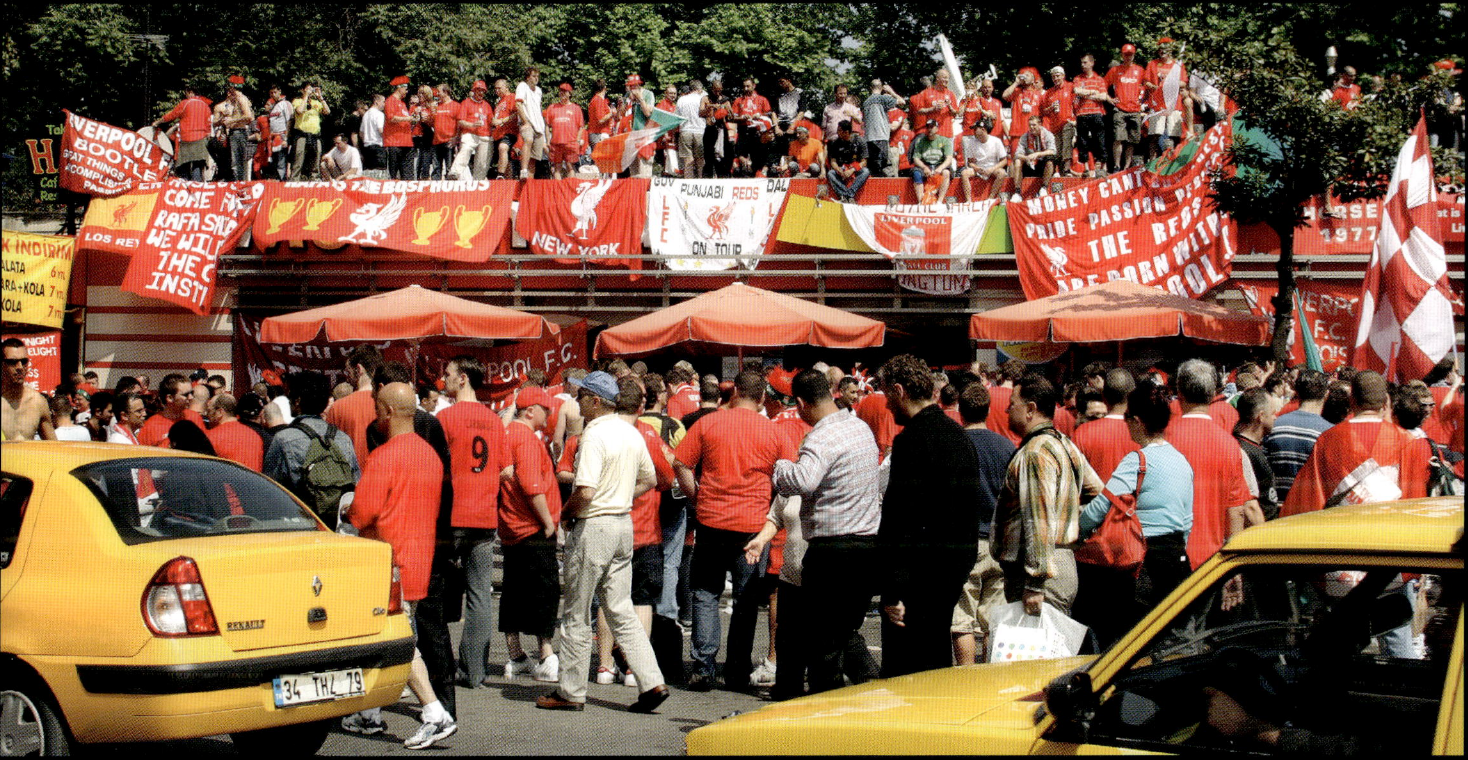
PUNJABI REDS
ON TOUR
NEW YORK
34 THL 79

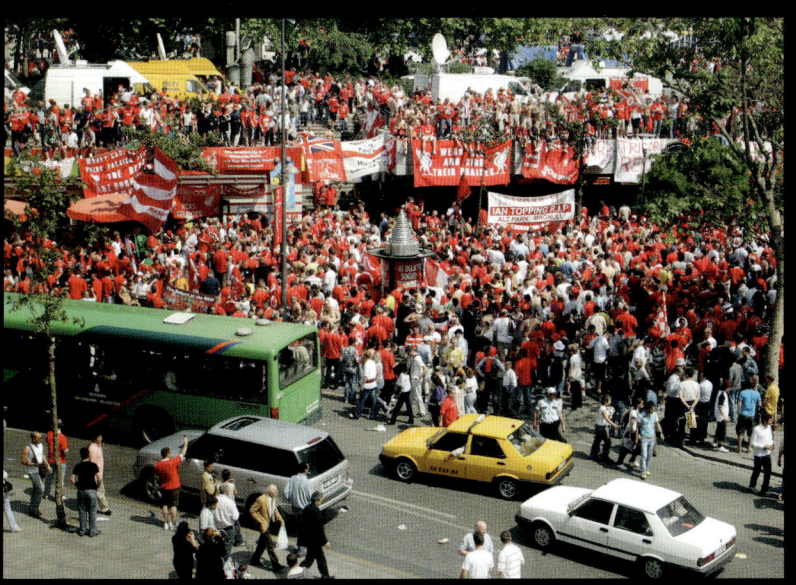

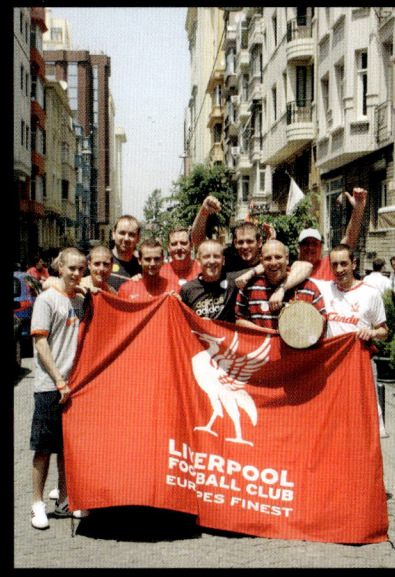

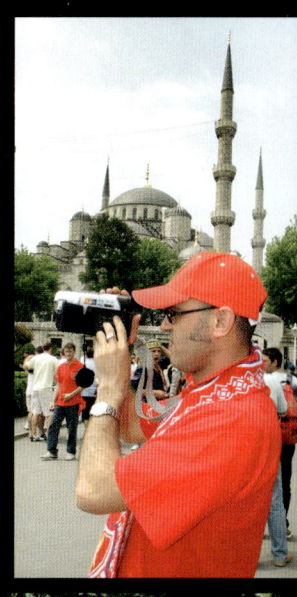

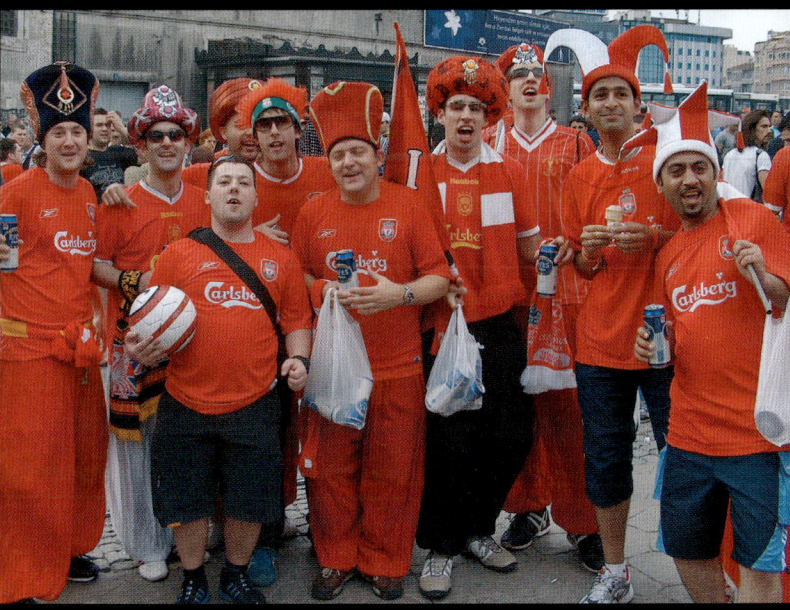

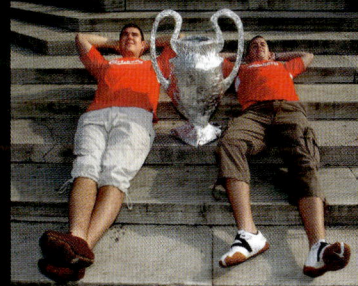

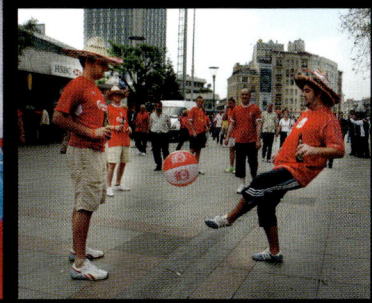

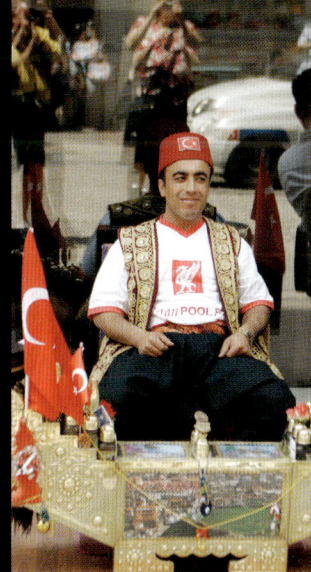

The travelling Kop arrives on the big stage. Picture: **Tony Woolliscroft**

CAPTAIN, MANAGER, CHAIRMAN AND CHIEF EXECUTIVE

Here's what key figures at LFC said in the hours following the Reds' fifth European Cup success

MANAGER: RAFAEL BENITEZ

Rafael Benitez admitted he faced the toughest job of his footballing life when he walked into the Liverpool dressing room at half-time with his team 3-0 down.

He may have been the only man in the Ataturk Stadium who believed the Reds were not a condemned team, but he was able to rouse his men for the comeback of all comebacks.

"It was very difficult to go into that dressing room and see the players with their heads down," he said. "We talked about different things. We had worked very hard for ten days and we needed to fight to the end. You have to keep believing in yourself.

"We had fought hard to be in the final. I was thinking about what to say and what to change. I needed to change the system and we needed to be more aggressive. I had to give confidence to the players.

"The first thing I did was explain the plan to Didi [Hamann]. I wasn't thinking about winning then, only about scoring. If we did that then Milan's reaction

could be very different. They were afraid and everything changed when we scored."

Immediately after the game, Rafa was still trying to absorb the magnitude of the achievement.

"I don't have words to express what I feel at the moment. You concede in the first minute, you lose Harry Kewell, players go down with cramp and it's very difficult. We tried to change things at half-time and said it would be different if we scored – and it was. But the players believed and we won. Steven Gerrard is a key player for us, he has the mentality."

Benitez, who stood unobtrusively to the side of the Liverpool squad on the podium as the trophy was handed over, tried to play down his own role in the achievement.

"As a manager you are important sometimes and you make mistakes, but the most important people are your staff and your players. Never call me the special one!

"I am one step closer to what the other [Liverpool] managers achieved, that's all. I have to do a lot more before I am considered on the same level."

"Lifting the trophy has to be the best feeling ever. How can I think of leaving Liverpool after a night like this?

"The supporters have saved up for weeks and months to come here. I am so happy to lift the cup for the fans.

"This is the greatest game I have played in. There can never have been anything like it before. Lifting the cup as Liverpool captain was just the best moment of my life.

"We were massive underdogs at the beginning of the competition and I'll put my hands up and say I didn't think we were going to go all the way. But, as you can see, we are never beaten.

"The manager told us to keep our chins up, to try and score early in the second half and give some respect for the fans.

"Milan had played the ball so quickly and so fluently and cleverly during that first half that it took a lot out of us chasing their shadows because we could not get near them. We were lucky to be only 3-0 down. Milan's football was world class.

"When I scored it started to change. That goal gave us a bit of belief. What happened next was amazing. How do you find words to describe it?

"When Jerzy made that double save from Shevchenko deep into extra time, just before he hit it, I thought 'goal', and I knew that would be the end of it but then when it went over the bar, I thought maybe it was going to be our day.

"In extra time, I spoke to a few of the lads on the pitch and we were all tired. I was running on empty even with 10 or 12 minutes of normal time still to go and admit I was thinking of penalties.

"Then when Serginho missed their first one I thought to myself again 'we are meant to win this'.

"I was down to take the fifth penalty so I was especially delighted when Jerzy saved from Shevchenko. The manager had asked me whether I wanted to take one and I said 'yes'. When he told me he had put me on the last one, I thought 'cheers'.

"How can anything follow a game like that?"

CAPTAIN: STEVEN GERRARD

CHAIRMAN: **DAVID MOORES**

Liverpool chairman David Moores revealed that football legend Michel Platini commiserated with him at half-time, believing Liverpool's only target in the second half would be to maintain respectability.

He said: "I was sitting near Platini and he came up to me at half-time and said 'I'm sorry, Mr Chairman, but your manager is going to have to do some damage limitation from this point.'

"Then he came up to me at full-time and said 'I must apologise. Your club has shown great courage. You should be proud of them.'

"I am. I'm proud of every player and supporter. No one thought we'd get this far at half-time against Olympiakos. Even when we were losing to Grazer in the qualifier

things didn't look good. We've been underdogs all the way."

Moores, who had been on the brink of standing down as chairman admitted the uncertainty surrounding his position had strained him.

"Everyone has difficult times and you just have to believe you're right and battle on.

"This club means the world to me and I'm not going to let it go easily.

"I admit the pressure was telling on me, but my wife had said to me 'What else would you do? This is your life.' It is.

"The grass-roots support has helped me through it all. You've got to keep going in life and a night like this is what this club is all about as far as I'm concerned."

"Our sensational victory in the Ataturk Stadium in Istanbul provided me with the greatest moment of my football life.

"I was delighted for the fans, the players and our manager Rafa Benitez who deserved this moment of glory after coming through a challenging first season at Anfield.

"Debate will continue as to whether this was the greatest European Cup final of all-time. What an achievement for the boys. For me, this success is up there with any of our previous glory days and that includes 1977, 1978, 1981 and 1984. The fact that our fifth triumph enables us to keep that most famous of trophies adds to it.

"I'm sure many thousands of you will have great pleasure in looking at it in future, be it displayed in our famous trophy room or in the Anfield Visitors' Centre.

It certainly won't be in the boardroom. It will be out on public display as a symbol of the part our supporters played in an incredible night in Turkey.

"I'm still in a state of shock. No one could believe the way we stared defeat in the face and came back so powerfully to force a penalty shoot-out.

"I'm still trying to take it all in. Like many of you, I didn't want to leave the stadium. At the same time I was aware of the scenes that were going on back in Liverpool as those who couldn't be with us began a very special city centre party that continued when we returned with the cup.

"Once again our fans did us proud. Magnificent in Istanbul, majestic on Merseyside, they helped everyone believe that anything is possible at LFC. We wanted to win that trophy for them. Let's just say it's 20 years overdue."

CHIEF EXECUTIVE: **RICK PARRY**

THE TRAVELLING KOP IN

İstanbul

Liverpool FC official matchday programme writer **CHRIS McLOUGHLIN** was among the press pack in Istanbul. Here's how he recounted the experience at the time

Was it all a dream? It was at the start of the season.But it turned to reality in Istanbul for thousands of Kopites...

'Above Us Only Sky' states the sign outside John Lennon iInternational Airport.

'Inside us only travelling Kopites' seems more appropriate in the (far too) early hours of May 25, 2005.

It's 3.53am on the morning of Liverpool's sixth European Cup final and the queues inside the airport are already building.

All the check in desks are open. All are busy. With over 4,000 Reds due to depart Speke for Istanbul in the space of two hours, it's hardly a surprise.

The pre-departure area is rammed. Wetherspoons is standing room only, while a presumably temporary shop full of Liverpool Champions League merchandise is doing roaring trade.

Standing outside it, dressed in a rather snappy suit, it is that bloke who was Jennifer Ellison's dad in Brookside. Can't think of his name although given the early hour I'm not entirely sure what my name is.

There's a huge queue for newspapers and snacks. WH Smiths is doing a roaring trade.

Copies of the Mirror, Star, Express, Mail, Sport and Daily Post, which are full of pre-match previews, are flying off the shelves like hot-cakes. Piles of the S*n remain untouched.

I manage to find a seat inside the 'Aintree Food Village' where my three, equally bleary-eyed LFC Magazine colleagues - Dave, Gav and Al - join me.

Turns out Jennifer Ellison's dad from Brookside is called Mark Moraghan and has also been in Holby City and Dream Team. Don't remember them getting to the European Cup final.

The lads have also spotted celebrity Evertonian John Parrott inside the airport. He's there along with his family awaiting a flight for their holiday destination.

"Going the match, John?" quips one of the airport's officials. "I'd rather have a leg off," he responds with a wry smile.

Imagine being a famous Blue in the same airport as 4,000 Kopites on the way to the final of the European Cup. He must be sick as a p.....ig.

Our flight is called and we join the queue to get through security.

A roll of stickers containing the Hillsborough flame and the slogan 'Don't Buy the S*n' is passed down the line. Everyone takes one.

Passports are checked, bags scanned and bodies frisked before we reach the departure lounge. It's like the concourse inside the Kop 15 minutes before a derby game.

The ale is already flowing, despite it being little after 5am, songs are ringing out and banners are draped everywhere.

We head through to our gate and get on a bus which takes us to our plane.

The plane has BLUELINE written on the side. Don't they do taxis and have an office on Oakfield Road?

We're kept waiting for a while as the plane is refuelled but on board the mood is good. The cabin crew are French. Wonder if they remember Paris '81?

Can't understand a word the captain is saying as we take off but then that doesn't matter. We're the greatest team in Europe and we really are on our way to Istanbul now.

Just under four hours later and we touch down in Istanbul at the city's Sabiha Gokcen airport on the Asian side of the city.

A bus meets us at the runway and drops us off at the terminal where we go through security. So much for needing a photocopy of our passports. The Turkish authorities hand them back without even looking at them and after stamping our passports we find our coach that takes us on the 70-minute journey to our hotel. Istanbul clearly has some poor areas.

As we drive towards the Bosphorus a sprawling mass of ramshackle and seemingly half-finished apartments and tiny shops provide a somewhat grim backdrop to the smog-choked motorway.

Most of the buildings are high-rise and in need of a lick of paint, yet almost all have a satellite dish sat on the balcony of each individual apartment. Clearly missing Fenerbahce v Galatasaray is unthinkable round these parts.

Every so often a beautifully designed and well-maintained mosque stands out among the high rises.

Other buildings are businesses containing more familiar logos such as Renault, Ford and Total.

As we approach the bridge over the Bosphorus I spot a giant furniture store that is simply called 'Rome'.

Thoughts of 1977 and 1984 immediately spring to mind. Looks like another good omen.

The scenery is breathtaking as we cross the Bosphorus. Fishermen stand on the bridge, their lines dangling towards the water, although given the number of boats out there you wonder if they're actually trying to hook up some cargo rather than cod.

With the sun shimmering on the water a more aesthetically pleasing view of the European side of Istanbul comes into view.

That's momentarily shattered when our coach driver is forced to slam on his breaks to avoid hitting a battered old van that has trundled into his path at a ludicrously slow speed.

Shock soon turns to laughter on the coach as we drive past the van and see that it's been driven by a bloke who looks so old that he was probably born in the city when it was called Constantinople.

The traffic gets a lot heavier as we head towards the heart of the city but it's not long before we are dropped off outside our hotel - the Kaya Hotel - in the suburb of Findikzade.

We don't check in. We've already been warned the day before that the hotel wasn't the best - Jamie Carragher's dad, Philly, stayed there last night and checked out after describing it as 'a hole' so our tour operator has managed to arrange us a transfer to another hotel.

We jump into the nearest cab outside, which was as easy as finding a penguin on the Falklands, and show our driver the address of the Hotel Gunes.

"OUR DRIVER IMMEDIATELY REVEALS HIMSELF TO BE A TURKISH AC MILAN FAN, WHICH EXPLAINS THE RED, WHITE AND BLACK SHIRT HE'S GOT ON"

It's now that we realise how truly crazy the roads in Istanbul are.

There appear to be no rules other than don't wear a seat belt, drive at whatever speed you want, beep your horn repeatedly and ensure you cut up your fellow motorist at any available opportunity. Pedestrians run the same risks that hedgehogs do in England.

Arriving at our new hotel we bump into the Liverpool Echo's David Prentice who is off to sample the delights of a Turkish bath. Well, he didn't used to get out in Europe much when he was covering the Blues.

Then the problems start. Our hotel had never heard of us. There was no record of our booking, no nothing.

An hour of frantic phone calls later and our tour operator (who had failed to reserve our rooms), and a Turkish travel agency, have managed to find us a couple of rooms at the Marble Hotel near Taksim Square.

We're told that it's only 20 minutes away so with the time now approaching 4pm at least we'll have time to join the party at Taksim Square and get a few much needed bevvies. Or so we think.

As we leave the Gunes Hotel the security guard offers to sort us out with a taxi and promptly runs off round the corner, which was nice.

Moments later he returns in cab and as he gets out - with a few lira from the driver for his troubles - we get in.

Our driver immediately reveals himself to be a Turkish AC Milan fan, which explains the red, white and black shirt he's got on.

He sparks up and offers us all a cig which even my two smoking colleagues refuse, largely because the smoke coming out of it is so strong that it even overpowers the smell of pollution coming in through the windows.

After five minutes of telling us in broken English how Milan are going to win, how Liverpool are 'not so good' and saying 'Shevchenko' more often than Peter Crouch says 'ow, me head' when he walks through a door, we approach one of Istanbul's many traffic jams.

'Traffic problem' he says pointing at the queue. 'Big problem'.

He then starts pointing at a completely clear road to our right and suggests that it is a short-cut before deciding to reverse back down what appears to be the equivalent of the M6 to get to the turn off, which was a bit concerning.

It's not long before we hit traffic again and this time we are stuck in it.

Still banging on about Milan, our driver has now taken to driving up alongside coaches carrying Rossonere supporters and beeping his horn at them, waving and laughing manically to himself.

Only the sound of hardcore dance music on his radio distracts him and as we crawl slowly towards Taksim Square our taxi now sounds like a mobile version of the 051. It'll be sunrise before we get to the game at this rate.

An hour-and-a-half after beginning our '20 minute' journey and we finally arrive at Taksim Square.

It's a hive of activity and an Anfield stronghold.

The square itself, which isn't exactly square, is lined by bars, restaurants, shops, hotels and parked taxis.

It's also got so much traffic pouring through it that it's a minor miracle none of the thousands of boisterous Reds who are spilling out on to the roads have been mowed down.

There are Liverpool banners all over the place and thousands of well oiled voices making themselves, and the Kop's anthems, well and truly heard.

We pay the driver (who has clearly made a mint out of us), find our hotel and the check-in staff are so pleased to see us that they insist we all have a room each which contain a total of nine beds.

It's now 6pm and we're hearing stories of how it's taking over two hours to get to the Ataturk Stadium.

Given that we have to pick up our tickets at the ground - and no later than 8.30pm or we can't get in - then the only option is to abandon the pre-match pint(s) and get straight up there.

So it's into another taxi and off to the stadium.

The traffic is slow but moving — until we get within a few miles of the ground. Then it becomes clear why it's taking so long.

Access to the stadium is by two single, one-lane roads that wind round the biggest building site you could ever wish to see.

Actually, calling it a building site doesn't really do it justice because there is no building work taking place.

It's wasteland. Desolate, barren and piled so high that it hid the stadium from view. The only thing on it is the odd Turkish Police officer, keeping an eye on the snarl up.

"WE'RE IN THE THIRD TIER OF THE WEST STAND, PRETTY MUCH ON THE HALF-WAY LINE. TO OUR LEFT IS A SEA OF RED WITH HUNDREDS OF BANNERS LAID OUT ON THE RUNNING TRACK IN FRONT OF IT. TO OUR RIGHT A SEA, WELL, MORE LIKE A STREAM OF RED, BLACK AND WHITE WITH BANNERS LAID OUT IN FRONT OF IT"

The taxis and coaches were now occupying both the incoming and outgoing lanes from the stadium - which makes life difficult for anyone trying to get away from it - and a cab full of Liverpool fans with very Southern accents pulls up alongside us.

They lean out their windows, start singing that they 'were going to Istanbul' (despite already being here) and give us a bit of stick before suddenly realising that we aren't Milanese as they'd initially thought.

Clearly getting out of Plymouth is very exciting for them.

Like almost everyone else stuck in the queue we decide to get out and walk the final mile to the stadium.

The stadium looks impressive as we approach it and, thankfully, we reach our ticket collection point with half-an-hour to spare before taking a quick walk round.

Thousands of Reds are outside the ground, behind the North Stand, where a giant screen is showing footage of the run to the final and an almighty sing-song is taking place. There is also a giant stage but little else to see or do except for a few 'game zones' that have been set up by Sony PlayStation.

There's nowhere to buy food and nowhere to buy drink unless you're a VIP who can get access to a giant marquee that's been set up. Even the programmes appear to have sold out. Ridiculous.

Getting into the stadium takes a while as the barcode entry system to our area is more temperamental than Basil Fawlty's car but finally we are in.

The Ataturk Stadium itself is a disappointment. It's nothing special inside.

The running track around the pitch makes you feel like you're a million miles away from the action and the grey seats aren't exactly inspirational.

Even the acoustics are poor because most of the stadium, save for the giant West Stand and the top of the East Stand, are uncovered. Again, it's impossible to buy even a bottle of water inside the ground unless you're in the VIP or press areas.

Exactly how can this be considered a venue worthy of holding a Champions League final?

We're in the third tier of the West Stand, pretty much on the halfway line. To our left is a sea of red with hundreds of banners laid out on the running track in front of it. To our right a sea, well, more like a stream of red, black and white with banners laid out in front of it.

It's obvious that the stadium is three quarters Liverpool. We're at home in a European final. Again.

If Anfield is in Merseyside and Anfield South is in Cardiff (at least while Wembley Stadium is being redeveloped!) then Anfield East is in Istanbul.

The Milan players enter the arena first to a cacophony of boos. Rafa's Redmen follow them out and receive a heroes welcome before an impromptu rendition of You'll Never Walk Alone begins.

All the noise is coming from the travelling Kop who are soon twirling their scarves again, à la Chelsea at home, while the evening sky is sporadically lit up by red flares.

The pre-match entertainment sees a load of kids in red trample across the Liverpool banners behind the goal. They are hastily removed by stewards (the banners, not the kids).

Finally the Milan fans wake up and reveal a giant banner, featuring a giant devil with the words 'Pensiero Stupendo' on it.

The translation is 'marvellous thought'. Well, Liverpool winning the European Cup tonight is.

The way they organised themselves into strips of red, white and black is impressive and as they all wave flags in unison it becomes clear that we are up against Italy's version of the Kop.

On the pitch we were just up against it.

There's no need to relive the first half. Utter dejection is the half-time mood. Gutted.

Three-nil down and the way Milan are playing we'll be lucky to get nil.

A text from my brother Andy, who is in the North Stand, simply says 'It doesn't get any worse than this'.

I can't help but feel he had sent it 45 minutes too early. The Milan players congratulate each other as they leave the pitch at half-time while their fans celebrate and unveil a giant red and black banner that says FORZA MILAN COMMANDOS TIGRE.

The translation? They think they've won. So do some Reds who have already headed for the exit.

Then, from somewhere, comes a murmur of You'll Never Walk Alone. Soon the murmur becomes a defiant statement.

It's a stunning show of support and belief which is followed by a chant of 'we're gonna win 4-3'. I turn to Gav and, with my tongue in my cheek, say that if we haven't made it 3-3 by the hour then we're in trouble.

The Milan players swagger their way back on to the pitch. Gennaro Gattuso comes on raising his fist in the air in celebration. Arrogant git. Come on Reds, get at 'em.

With Didi on we look better. Stevie is driving us forward and scores in the 54th minute. Yes. Gerrin' there. We've got half a chance.

Two minutes later and the ball falls to Vladi 25 yards out. Bang. It's 3-2. Game on. Can you believe it?

Three quarters of the ground go ballistic. The Milan fans are silent.

We've barely caught out breath and Stevie goes down in the box. PENALTY! Yeeeeeeeees.

Everyone's heads are going. Carra's going mad at the ref for not showing Gattuso red. Alonso's stepping up to take it.

Saved. No. Rebound. Yes! I'm up out of my seat in the press area with my arms in the air, much to the disgust of some stiff upper-lipped members of the national press. Sod 'em.

I look to my left and Dave is going mad too, while Spanish journalist Guillem Balague has managed to stay in his seat but is shaking both his fists in the air as if he's just seen his beloved Espanyol score the winner in the Nou Camp.

The travelling Kop are in raptures. The sea of red looks like it could flood on to the running track at any minute and wash Milan away.

WE SHALL NOT WE SHALL NOT BE MOVED is bellowed out with unshakeable belief.

Suddenly John Arne Riise lines up a shot. You can almost hear a collective gasp of breath as he hits it but Dida saves. No matter. The noise is still deafening.

The final half-hour of the second half passes in a blur. Despite it being the most exciting European Cup final ever, UEFA decide at this point to announce over the PA system that match-day programmes can be bought at the airport. Priorities, priorities.

The full-time whistle goes to loud cheers from the travelling Kop.

There's still extra-time to play but given how demoralised we all felt at half-time, it feels like we've won now.

The Liverpool Echo's Chris Bascombe and Roy Gilfoyle are both smiling. I can't see any Italian journalists doing the same. They look like they've just seen their team blow an unassailable 3-0 lead and had to rip up their back-page stories.

Extra-time starts and it's clear we're knackered. Milan are on top again but are struggling to create anything.

Carra makes a brilliant block and goes down with cramp. You can actually see the spasms in both his legs. He really is playing through the pain barrier for us.

Two minutes from time and Shevchenko gets a free header. Jerzy saves but it falls back to the European Footballer of the Year who is two yards out with the big Pole in our goal on the floor.

Hearts sink. Dreams shatter. So near but so far.

But that's in the Milan end.

Jerzy has somehow managed to flick the ball over the bar.

How? No-one knows but we aren't half glad. If he's producing Gordon Banks-esque saves like that then you've got to fancy him on pens.

The whistle goes and it's spot-kicks.

Maldini wins the toss. It's down at their end and Stevie chooses for them to take first. Just like in 1984.

The tension is unbearable. If you'd offered me on the opening day of the season a place in the Champions League final and a penalty shoot-out against AC Milan to decide it, I'd have bitten your hand off. Now the only thing being bitten are my nails.

Serginho steps up.

'Miss you b*****d' isn't probably considered as exemplary press-box etiquette but then watching Liverpool take part in a penalty

shoot-out in the Champions League final didn't crop up when I was at college and I'm watching history in the making, not my p's and q's.

Jerzy dances round on the line and Serginho does as I ask.

Yes! It's a great start for us. It gets even better when Didi exorcises his personal ghost of the 2001 Worthington Cup final and makes it 1-0.

Next up is Pirlo, Milan's dead-ball expert.

Jerzy is dancing round his line and again and... he's saved it. Yeeees! Looks like he moved a bit early but the ref's ok with it. If Cisse puts this one in it's well on for us.

Come on Djibril lad... yeeeeeeees. 2-0. An emphatic finish. We're so close now.

Tomasson makes it 2-1 and next up is Riise. He goes for placement instead of power and Dida guesses right. Damn. Not to worry though, Ginge lad. We're still 2-1 up.

Kaka walks forward and Jerzy is now wobbling his legs like Brucie Grobbelaar did in '84 and doing star-jumps.

Kaka's been that good today though that surely he won't miss?

He doesn't. 2-2. The kid's a class act.

Vladi is the next man forward. Some Reds are worried. I'm not. I've seen him take them before and he's good from the spot. 3-2. No problemo.

That means Shevchenko must score to keep Milan in it. As he steps forward I think of two things.

One. The look of utter shock on his face when Jerzy kept him out with that wonder save just moments ago that said 'it's not my day'.

Two. Roberto Baggio. The best player in World Cup '94 but the man who missed the penalty in the final to hand Brazil the trophy.

Now if the best player in Europe misses from 12 yards out it will hand us the trophy.

He's gonna be the new Baggio, I'm thinking to myself. And when he is I'm gonna write about it.

And so I have.

Jerzy does the business again and Liverpool are champions of Europe. Yeeeeeeeeeeeeeeeeeeeeeeeeeee eeeeeeeeeeeeeeeeeeeeeeeeeeeeeeeeeeeeeees!

I've never leapt out of a press seat so quickly. All I remember

now is hugging Dave who is saying over and over again 'we're the champions of Europe' as if he can't believe it and tears stinging my eyes.

On the pitch and around three quarters of the ground it's utter pandemonium. The celebrations are the wildest and most ecstatic I've ever witnessed. It all seems so surreal.

The younger generation of Reds have only ever read about nights like this. Now we're experiencing it first hand. I don't want it to end.

Then comes the moment none of us were sure we'd ever see in the flesh. Steven Gerrard, captain of Liverpool Football Club, is (finally) handed the European Cup and raises it high towards the heavens.

The roar that goes up almost drowns out the Champions League theme tune and what seems like a tonne of red ticker-tape is blasted into the sky from behind the stage.

Now it's believable. Now it's real. That's Liverpool's captain with the European Cup in his hands. It's a moment to savour. A moment to cherish. A moment of sheer exultation. A moment that I will never, ever forget.

As the celebrations continue into what is going to be a night that you can see lasting right the way through until August, it's time for my colleagues and I to temporarily come back down to earth.

We've got press conferences to attend, interviews to conduct and reports to write. Our first sip of anything remotely alcoholic must wait.

It's almost 4am by the time we reach our hotel after the game. Taksim Square is buzzing. It seems like a lot of locals have now joined the jubilant travelling Kopites and the bars are rammed again.

There's red everywhere and hoarse Scouse voices are competing with taxi horns to make themselves heard.

We've still got work to do - this LFC Mag doesn't write itself - but there is no way on earth we're not having a bevvie now so it's straight to the hotel bar.

The barman rustles up four bottles of Carlsberg and we make a toast to the new Champions of Europe. Campioni Liverpool.

By 5.30am, and several bottles of Tuborg later, the reality that we still had work to do hits home so it was back to our rooms and out with the laptops.

For some reason reception give me a wake up call at 6.15am, which would have been useful if I'd actually been to sleep by then, and in the end I get about an hour-and-a-half's worth of kip. Some of the lads get less.

The party is still going outside when I wake up. A cleaner is sat on the stairs outside my room, waiting patiently to clean a room that I've spent less time in than I did on the plane.

We leave and get a taxi back up to the Kaya Hotel where the coach taking us back to the airport is waiting for us.

Our travel steward, a thoroughly decent and helpful guy, tells us that there is chaos at the airport and there are delays of five hours and more. As a result we're staying at this hotel until 1.30pm.

That gives us a couple of hours to kill and the chance to finally get some scran. By now I've gone past the point of being hungry but eating seems like a good idea.

Dave and Gav go for a kebab. As Dave put it, after biting into what he can only describe as 'mystery meat', "well it LOOKED alright".

Al settles for a spam roll and I order what looks like a cross between a bagel and a pasty which they stick in an oven.

I have no idea what's inside it. It looks like cheese but the taste is new to me.

I'd rather not know and eat as much as it as physically possible. At least it was cheap.

We wander around the shops and I buy a Turkish paper which has the Liverpool players on the front and the headline 'Destanpool' on it. Don't understand a word of it but it's a nice souvenir.

By 2.30pm we're back at Sabiha Gokcen Airport or, to be more precise, in a giant marquee that's sat on the car park outside of it.

It's full of weary-looking Reds. Many have been there all night. With the game finishing late the roads being chaotic and stories that the taxi drivers had deliberately delayed coaches to try and get the fans off them and into their cabs, most had missed their flights last night which had taken off without them because they had to fly in their allotted airtime.

Chaos reins. The airport authorities can't cope with the thousands of people there and some fans have been shoved on the first plane that comes, wherever they were going to.

A giant departure board in the centre of the tent lists 15 flights. 14 have 'delay' next to them. Only the flight to Cairo says 'on time'. Looks like the Egyptian supporters club have struck lucky then.

I speak to one lad whose flight hasn't even made the board yet. Hopefully he's back by now.

Cynicism is rife. The marquee is full of bars and stalls selling beer, food, papers, gifts and souvenirs at vastly inflated prices. They are charging 10 new Turkish Lira (£4) for a copy of The Times or a pint. It feels like it's been planned.

Thankfully the mood is still good because Liverpool have won. If we'd lost then it could have been nasty.

We're told we've got a four-hour delay.

That makes us lucky. We hear that others could be stuck here until Sunday night.

All of a sudden there's a big cheer and fans rush towards a bloke who's just walked in.

It's John Aldridge. The fans swarm round him, taking pictures on their mobiles and chanting his name.

Aldo is hoisted up into the air and shakes his first in joyous celebration and shouts something that I can't make out. A huge cheer follows and he's ushered through the crowds into the airport to wait for his flight.

We're finally called to board our plane and, after managing to convince an over-zealous security officer that the buckle on my belt keeps setting his alarm off because it's made of metal and I'm not hiding an illegal weapon, I'm allowed through to board the plane.

We take off at 6.15pm. It should have been 2pm, but by now I'm happy just to be on a plane home.

The in-flight meal doesn't touch the sides but, try as I might, I can't sleep when I'm flying. Never can.

We land (at the second attempt) at about 8.30pm and I switch my mobile on to receive a flurry of texts telling me how fantastic the homecoming is and that hundreds of thousands of people are out on the streets.

What should I do - try and get down to St George's Hall or go home? I'm still debating the point when I get to my car and hear on Radio City that the bus is on Scottie Road and the city centre and all routes leading to it are jammed.

Time for my head to rule my heart.

I go home and watch what is left of the parade on BBC News 24. My mates down there keep me informed of what it's like.

Anyway, being there in Istanbul on the night Liverpool won and got to keep the European Cup is the main thing for me.

I arrive home tired and hungry, but still absolutely jubilant. It's been a long trip to end a long season but it's all been worth it.

What an experience. What a comeback. What a night.

I don't think it gets any better than this but then I'm sure the travelling Kopites returning from Rome in 1977 thought the same thing and that was only the start of our European dynasty.

For now I'm just happy with the one cup and, as things stand, there's only one way I can describe May 25, 2005.

Best night of my life.

> ## "I DON'T THINK IT GETS ANY BETTER THAN THIS BUT THEN I'M SURE THE TRAVELLING KOPITES RETURNING FROM ROME IN 1977 THOUGHT THE SAME THING AND THAT WAS ONLY THE START OF OUR EUROPEAN DYNASTY"

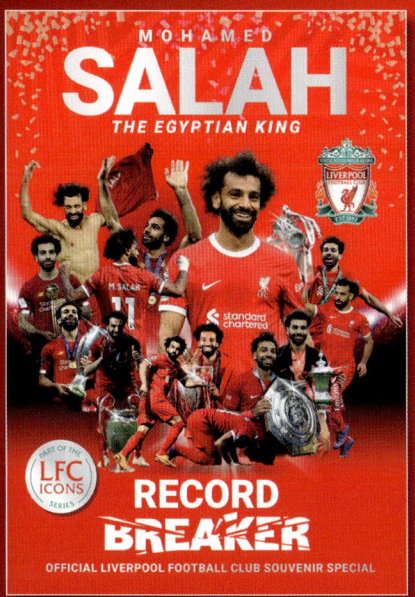
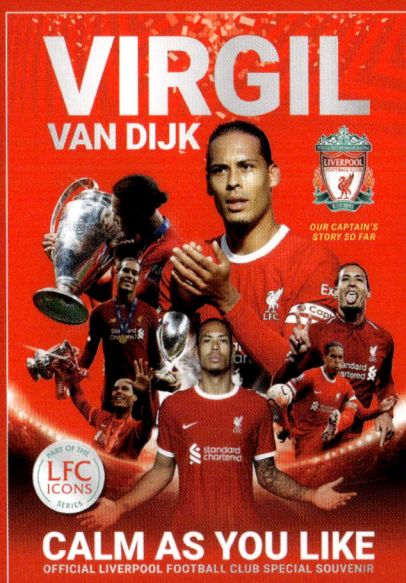
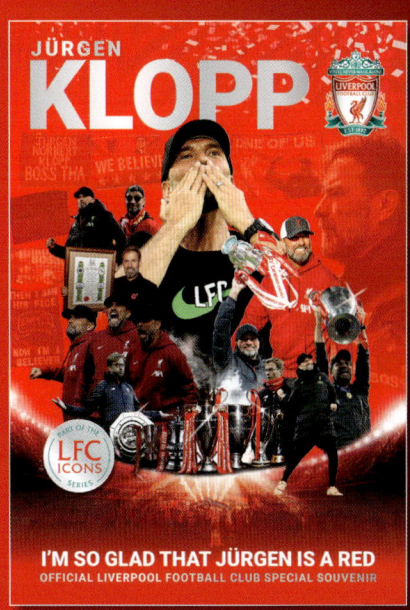
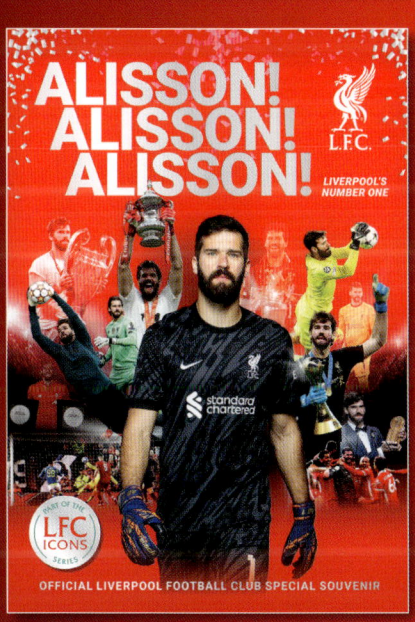
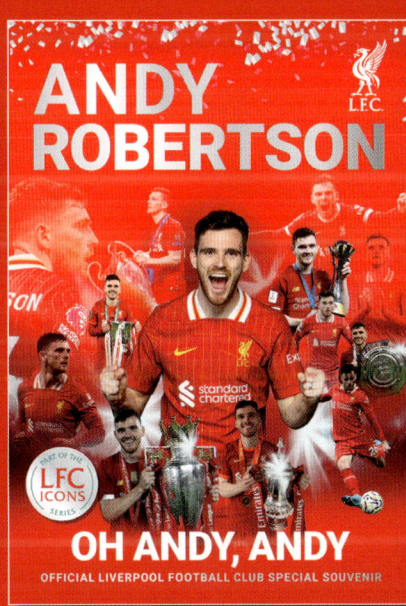
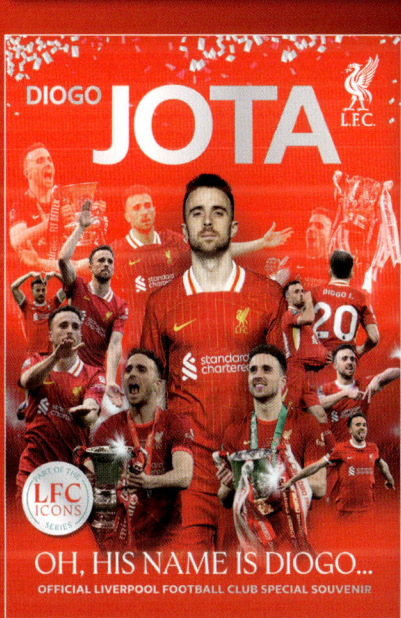

HELLO – HELLO – HERE WE GO!

CLIVE TYLDESLEY, whose words are part of the folklore of that night at the Ataturk, relives what he was thinking, feeling and saying when the Liverpool goals went in

AS TOLD TO **DAVID COTTRELL**

always avoid questions about the best game that I've ever seen or the best goal or the best player, because I believe that football belongs in its moment. Football's power over us is that it defines moments and years in our lives. We remember who we watched the great games with, who we celebrated or commiserated with.

To this day, for everything that Liverpool have achieved since 2005, that final against AC Milan in Istanbul remains the single greatest and most talked-about memory in the lives of a generation of Liverpool fans. And because the narrative of the night was so full of surprises and the proverbial twists and turns, I would say that it's the most memorable match I've ever commentated on.

That doesn't mean it was the best. I honestly believe that the Liverpool team that lined up against Milan two years later was a stronger team and produced a better performance, and lost the final. But whoever came up with the phrase, 'You couldn't write it'

must have seen this game because so many of the heroes in 2005 were unlikely heroes, so many of the events could not have been predicted.

Right down until the final penalty being taken by one of the stars of the world game at the time in Andriy Shevchenko, and Jerzy Dudek who, if we are totally honest, had had a mixed night and was on his way out, makes the save. If we link that with Djimi Traore's goal-line clearance and Vladimir Smicer's delayed arrival from the bench and the impact that he had on the game, in terms of a story, in terms of a mystery, in terms of a wonder, this game is beyond any kind of explanation or analysis.

Steven Gerrard played in three or maybe four different positions during the evening. It was his defining performance as a Liverpool player and captain, but you could argue that his finest 20 or 30 minutes were at right-back in extra-time against Serginho.

When I look back on it now and relive my tiny part in it, when for some reason I decided to say "Hello hello" after Gerrard's goal, it was a reflection on how Liverpool had got to Istanbul in the first

place. Via the late goals against Olympiakos [in the group stage], via an unlikely left-footed Sami Hyypia goal against Juventus [in the quarter-final first leg] and that fabulous second from Luis Garcia, via the 'ghost goal' against Chelsea and the whole furore around it, and despite being fifth in the Premier League. There was just a 'Wait a minute – these guys haven't quite finished this cup run yet'. And so it turned out.

I'm not a believer in fate but there was an element of their name being written on the trophy some weeks or months before, and I actually think that fed into Milan's reaction to those famous six minutes. Milan had been ambushed the year before by Deportivo and knocked out of the competition in bizarre circumstances [losing 4-0 in the quarter-final second leg after winning the first 4-1]. They'd almost been ambushed by PSV in the 2005 semi-finals [going through on away goals after it was 3-3 on aggregate].

Despite the galaxy of experienced stars that they had at their disposal, their Achilles heel was maybe a mental vulnerability to comebacks and crazy events – and there was certainly a crazy comeback that night. I can't tell you that it rocked them to their foundations because after Xabi had equalised Milan took control of the game again and it needed Djimi's clearance and Jerzy's ridiculous save to even get Liverpool to the shoot-out. But it must have fed into their mental state.

In a strange sort of way, my abiding image of the night is the look on Shevchenko's face when he walked forward and he didn't want to be there, he didn't want to be taking the next kick of the penalty shoot-out, and it was almost as if he knew what was going to happen because of what had happened in the previous two hours. In the end Liverpool got inside Milan minds with the sheer spirit and daring of their performance on the night.

For this season's Carabao Cup final at Wembley I was commentating for CBS Sport and the weirdest thing happened when Federico Chiesa pulled one back. I said, "Hello" and had to stop myself from saying the second 'hello'. The prospect of a Liverpool comeback against Newcastle at that point was unlikely but something in my psyche thought: I've seen this one before.

It's maybe not what Liverpool fans want to read, but what I said when Stevie scored takes me back to the first leg of a European Cup Winners' Cup semi-final that Liverpool played against PSG at Parc de Princes in 1997. It was a 3-0 defeat that night. I was commentating and it's probably the only time I can remember a boss of mine saying in my ear, "Come on, we've got the second leg next week."

As Liverpool went two-down I'd pretty much condemned them to defeat because of the nature of the performance that they were giving. And quite rightly my head of football, who is sadly not with us anymore, Jeff Farmer, told me to build it back up a bit, that they weren't out yet. I responded dutifully and tried to talk it up for the next few minutes until Liverpool conceded the third goal. At Anfield they nearly did get it back, it finished 2-0 but the second goal came just too late.

So when Steven headed the Riise cross in, I almost felt duty-bound to give it a chance, even though there was very little prospect of two more goals coming in the next 60 minutes, let

"IN TERMS OF A STORY, IN TERMS OF A MYSTERY, IN TERMS OF A WONDER, THIS GAME IS BEYOND ANY KIND OF EXPLANATION OR ANALYSIS"

alone the next six. I also think that element of 'And so it is written', about Liverpool's path to the final, resonated with me at that moment. You couldn't put it past these guys to find a way out of this hole that they've dug.

Because of the nature of the third Milan goal, the beauty of it, and the dominance that they'd established – although it was only really in the final 15 minutes of the first half that they'd started to outclass Liverpool – I did spend part of half-time checking through my records for record defeats for Liverpool and big defeats in European Cup finals. Someone recently asked me if I was aware of the fans singing 'You'll Never Walk Alone' at half-time and I said honestly no – I was too busy looking for when Liverpool last lost by eight goals because it did seem to be heading that way. I remembered 1960 and Real Madrid 7 Eintracht Frankfurt 3 at Hampden Park.

My great mentor in commentary was the late Reg Gutteridge who took me under his wing, and he always demanded that if you are fortunate enough to witness something unique, you need to come up with some unique words to match it because 'amazing', 'brilliant', 'fantastic' are not enough.

After Smicer scored the second it was part of my process to conjure up some words in my mind if they got another. So I think "Mission Impossible is accomplished" was dreamt-up in the couple of minutes between the second and third goals. I'd started to ask myself the editorial question: what's the headline if they equalise? I had Andy Townsend alongside me, who was one of the best operators I've ever worked with and would always give you some thinking time. Reg always used to say that silence is golden for a commentator but you're not resting, you're thinking – you're thinking what comes next.

People ask about the words and whether you scripted them the day before. You can't. There's absolutely no way. I remember going through the same process with the Dejan Lovren goal against Dortmund [in the 2016 Europa League quarter-final second leg]. You want to come up with some words if it happens – and

> ## "PEOPLE ASK ABOUT THE WORDS AND WHETHER YOU SCRIPTED THEM THE DAY BEFORE. YOU CAN'T. THERE'S ABSOLUTELY NO WAY"

somehow it's more likely to happen at the Kop end at Anfield than in the wilds of Istanbul. And by the way, I always say to people that final was not in Istanbul. If you think it was in Istanbul, you didn't go – it was nowhere near Istanbul!

Funnily enough, the commentary line I'm most pleased about whenever I revisit Istanbul is "This time it's for keeps", when the trophy went up.

Having been at Radio City during European Cups one, two, three and four, the whole 'five times' thing was a big part of the narrative of the night.

Is Istanbul the most iconic Liverpool moment of the modern era? It's an interesting thing to throw at Liverpool fans and I guess you'll get a different answer from a 15-year-old than you will from a 55-year-old. In the April of 1977 I'd arrived on Merseyside – a Manc on Merseyside – just a few days before David Fairclough's goal against St Etienne. I do think that Rome was a huge breakthrough for Liverpool fans of a certain generation – and in many ways I don't think it will ever be beaten. It was a different kind of European Cup final because Liverpool were magnificent on the night and thoroughly deserved the victory over Borussia Moenchengladbach.

The thing is, Istanbul happened in isolation, it wasn't the beginning of anything, whereas 1977 was. That team under Bob Paisley that I was lucky enough to watch on a weekly basis, and the players I got to know as great friends, they never topped 77, even winning it at Wembley and beating Roma in Rome. So I suppose if you're of a certain generation you'd make an argument for that.

The other day someone said to me that Barcelona in 2019 takes some beating and I can see that because it happened at Anfield and was the product of greatness – arguably a much better Liverpool team than played in 2005. The defining moment for

Jürgen's team was the fourth goal, just the ingenuity of it. You talk about Liverpool greats on the field at the same time, there are three or four contenders for an all-time Liverpool XI who were on the field that night against Barcelona. But what was Istanbul? It was Jamie and Stevie and 'stick' – and somehow they found a way.

For pure romance and meaning and significance, of all the moments that Liverpool have given us in the modern era, I do think that Istanbul is still top of the charts. I said something else in the commentary when there was a shot of the Liverpool fans celebrating at the end, that they'd had to listen to their fathers and grandfathers going on about Shankly and Paisley and Dalglish and all the great teams, and now they had a champion team of their own. Perhaps there was a bit of that too.

Do I talk about it much? I don't really indulge myself in what's gone before. Liverpool are still winning trophies so you talk about the here and now because football belongs in its moment. I work pretty regularly with Jamie Carragher now on CBS for their Champions League coverage and I count him as a friend. But do we talk about 2005? No, there's too much to talk about in 2025, particularly around Liverpool. We talk about Liverpool, but we talk about this Liverpool.

Funnily enough before this season's Carabao Cup final at Wembley I also bumped into Jaap Stam, who of course played for Milan that night in Istanbul. He's a friend too because I live quite close to Reading whom he managed for a while. And no, as you might imagine, I didn't talk to him about it either!

• Follow Clive on X @CliveTyldesley

CLIVE'S COMMENTARY

3-1 "Charged down by Cafu...in towards
GERRAAARD!
Hello – hello – here we go!
Steven Gerrard puts a grain of doubt in the back of Milan minds and gives hope to all the many thousands of Liverpool fans."

3-2 "Hit by Smicer
IT'S IN! IT'S IN!
Vladimir Smicer! Two goals in two minutes for Liverpool!"

3-3 "Carragher into Baros he's laid it off it's
**GERRARD! HE WAS HELD!
HE'S GIVEN A PENALTY! HE'S GIVEN
THE PENALTY...**

Step up Xabi Alonso with the chance to equalise – yes, equalise – for Liverpool. Oh saved by Dida
XABI ALONSOOO!
And Mission Impossible is accomplished! Liverpool were three-nil down five minutes ago and now look at that scoreline!"

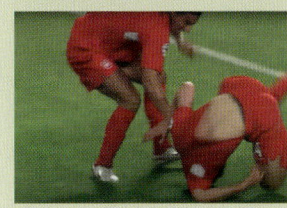 

THE MANAGERIAL
MASTERMIND

To the singing Kopites he is the legend they call Ra-fa, Ra-fa-el! To history he will always be known as the tactical genius who conquered Europe in his first season at Liverpool. The man who somehow turned back time at Anfield and inspired his players to pull back a 3-0 half-time deficit against the mighty Milan

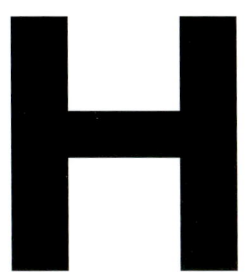

Hours before Liverpool played Juventus in Turin, Rafael Benitez was seen shopping for Lego. Benitez must be good at it, given the way he created a European Cup-winning team without having all the pieces he would want in place.

He has a weakness for puzzles that require careful planning. An ability to plan tactics and understand every detail was first demonstrated when playing the board game 'Stratego' as a 12-year-old in Madrid.

The aim of the game is to get your military commanders to capture the opponents' flags. Rafa was most upset when he lost to a friend and set about ensuring he never did so again, as he explained to bemused English journalists in March 2005.

"I stayed up all night thinking about why I'd lost and how I could prevent it happening again," he revealed.

"Once I'd learned the rules and understood the strategies, I didn't lose again. I worked out a way to win no matter who I played."

Even as a child, Benitez was fascinated by planning and analysing. Aged 13, "I would write in a book the names of the [Real] Madrid players and give them all marks". He would soon do the same in matches in which he was taking part.

By 18 he was player-manager of a university side. He oversaw them at a tournament and while the opposition teams partied until daybreak, Benitez ensured his squad went home early. They won.

His own playing career was never more than an extended warm-up for what he really wanted to do: coach.

Benitez was at Real Madrid between 1974 and 1981 but never broke into the first team. After five unremarkable years at clubs in the lower divisions, a knee injury forced his retirement in 1986.

Aged 26, he began coaching the Castilla 'B' youth team, returning to Real Madrid in 1989 as coach of their Under-19 side. He made his way up the ladder, taking charge of their reserve side before being appointed assistant manager in 1994.

During this period, he also worked at the Abasota gymnasium in Madrid, utilising a degree in physical education. Here he met his future wife, Montse.

By the time he reached his mid-30s, Benitez was ready to become a fully-fledged coach of a professional team.

He began his managerial apprenticeship at Valladolid and Osasuna.

Circumstances were not in his favour at either club, however, and when he was given time he was able to shape winning teams.

Benitez took Extremadura and Tenerife into the Spanish Primera Liga, spending a year's sabbatical between the two jobs studying coaching methods at leading clubs throughout Europe, including AC Milan. Perhaps the Italians regret their hospitality now.

Valencia offered Benitez his first major managerial job, where he took over from Hector Cuper in 2001. He broke the Real Madrid-Barcelona duopoly that reigned in Spain, winning two league titles and one UEFA Cup in his three seasons at the Mestalla.

A deteriorating relationship with chief executive Manuel Llorente hastened his departure from Valencia and within a fortnight Benitez was unveiled as Liverpool's new manager.

He soon found a way into the affections of the club's supporters, signing exciting players and making Anfield on matchday a fun day out again.

His low-key but charming manner further endeared him to a foreign public.

The ingenious re-working of the 'La Bamba' lyrics to honour Benitez and his Spanish signings is just one example of the instant adoration he inspired. Joining supporters in an Irish bar in Cologne the night before Liverpool played Leverkusen added to a burgeoning legend.

Behind the warm smile lies a man fixated with winning football matches. He is obsessed with the sport and the small details that can separate the best from the rest. In training sessions, the various aspects of the game are broken down for intense preparation, and these drills are frequently stopped so he can make a tactical point. Video analysis of his team and opponents is conducted to an exhausting degree. Anyone who watched a Liverpool game in 2004/05 is well aware of how animated he is on the touchline, instructing almost constantly while the match is in progress.

Benitez is always thinking, always working.

He won the FA Cup with the Reds in 2006 and led them to another Champions League final against Milan in Athens in 2007. The Reds were edged out 2-1 that day despite producing a more controlled performance than in Istanbul.

Rafa later managed Inter Milan to the FIFA Club World Cup in 2010, Chelsea to the UEFA Europa League in 2012/13 and Napoli to the Coppa Italia in 2013/14.

On the rare occasions he switches off from football, he will engross himself in another game of strategy: chess. Even when the opponent has him virtually at checkmate, Rafa can still find a way to prevail, as any supporter of AC Milan will testify.

15 MINUTES TO WORK A MIRACLE

It was the most momentous half-time in LFC history – DAVID COTTRELL takes us through how those who were there remember what happened in the Ataturk dressing-room

Rafael Benitez

Less than 12 months after the final, with events still fresh in his mind, Rafa revisited the half-time dressing-room with UEFA Champions magazine in April 2006...

"It was difficult, really difficult. We'd had a plan. We started the game, conceded the first goal and Harry Kewell was injured. Okay, we needed to change the plan. Then we conceded the second goal and I was thinking about half-time, how to change things. Straight away we conceded the third. Now I was thinking I needed to change my notes!

"I walked to the changing room, hearing all the fans, and I said to the players, 'We need to work hard for these people. If we score a goal, maybe things will change'. Then I decided to change the system. I said, 'Traore, get showered. And Didi, get ready. We will play 3-4-2-1. This is the idea, okay? Come on boys [claps]. Let's start working'.

"Then I turned and Steve Finnan was on the treatment table and [physio] Dave Galley said we'd have to change Finnan for the second half. We'd made one change, Smicer for Kewell in the first half. So I said, 'Traore, you're back on. Finnan, get to the shower'. Finnan was disappointed but Traore was ready to carry on.

"I went to the tactics board and I was thinking: okay, I've got Smicer as a right winger but he's not the best getting back to defend and we've lost Finnan. So I said, 'We will use Cisse on the left in attack'. But they said, 'Hang on boss, that means we've got 12 players on the pitch'. So, forget Cisse! I already had Luis Garcia as a second striker.

"Then the physio said, 'We've got one minute [before the second half]'. So we changed to 3-4-2-1 but used different players, with three at the back [Carragher, Hyppia, Traore] to give us more control in midfield [Alonso, Hamann, Riise, Smicer – with Gerrard and Garcia just behind Baros].

"I tried to keep the competitive spirit in the team and thought that with any luck we could end up being the better team. We had good luck because we scored early. If we scored again soon, they would go down. We did and then we scored again.

"I switched Gerrard to right-back in extra-time. Shevchenko had that chance and we had a bit of good luck, but we worked to get it. I always knew winning the Champions League would be difficult, but my idea is to think about winning games, not trophies."

Dietmar Hamann

Midfielder Didi, whose second-half appearance proved so crucial, was asked for his half-time recollections by UEFA.com in 2023...

"It was probably the most empty I've felt in my career as a football player and [...] I didn't see a way back into the game. Rafael Benitez said we'd make a change. The reason for me coming on was to give Steven Gerrard the freedom to go a bit further forward because he was our biggest goal threat.

"Every time games got tight and got into a dog fight, there was no better team than us. I thought to myself: if we get it back to 3-2, let's see how they react. Yes, they are a world-class team, but sometimes even the best teams under pressure do make mistakes.

"So, from going in at half-time to standing on the touchline 15 minutes later, my mindset had completely changed. I didn't believe we could win it, but I was hoping – I was believing – at least we could give them a game."

Gennaro Gattuso

The Milan midfielder was interviewed by Spanish journalist Guillem Balague for the book A Season on the Brink – now reissued as a 20th anniversary edition – and refuted accusations that his team-mates thought they had it won...

"It's an insult to hear someone, whose name I don't remember, say that people like [Paolo] Maldini or [Alessandro] Costacurta were celebrating at half-time. In fact, Ancelotti in the half-time team-talk said he was worried and talked about continuing playing together, with the same intensity, just as it happened in the first half, because if an English team scores a goal, with their support, that leaves the game open again. I love English fans, they can help you change the most impossible situations."

Luis Garcia

In 2020 the Liverpool Echo asked the Kop cult favourite what he remembers about half-time in the dressing-room...

"It all looks a bit blurry now. I remember myself getting in and seeing all the players sitting trying to cool down, there were faces of frustration all around. We didn't play that bad, they were just too good.

"Rafa got us together to set a new tactic with Stevie Gerrard at the front with Xabi and Didi in the middle. 'Try to control the midfield, and we are going to have chances', he said. What he wanted from us was what we had been doing the whole season: to wait for our opportunities to arrive.

"The first half, we had played with our heart and had anxiety after conceding in the first minute. We did not play with our heads and we paid for it. I never thought about when it will be the comeback, I had so many things in my head.

"We were sitting in the dressing-room and we could clearly hear thousands of fans singing You'll Never Walk Alone. Can you imagine how that felt? They never give up, never let us walk alone through the storm."

Vladimir Smicer

In the Balague book, the Czech attacker simply had this to say...

"It was pretty chaotic for a few moments in there. I was asking, 'What do I have to do boss? Where will I be playing? Am I going to be playing wide? Will I be the right-back, or what?' Then we realised that the boss had written his second-half scheme with 12 players in the team!"

Djimi Traore

The left-back was so nearly sacrificed at the interval until circumstances compelled him to stay on the pitch. Five years ago he told his story to the Liverpool Echo...

"I was supposed to be [substituted] out, that story is true. Rafa wanted to make the changes to the team. My priority as a full-back was not to attack, it was to defend. But at 3-0 down we needed to be more offensive, so he tried to make a tactical decision to play Riise as a wing-back and play three at the back.

"It was the right thing to do, but then Rafa found out Steve Finnan couldn't keep going. Because he had already used a sub with Harry Kewell, he couldn't use them all. He made the decision quickly. He said: 'Djimi, you stay in – Finnan is out' and Hamann came on to make sure we were well-balanced in the middle. He was asked to take care of Kaka who had hurt us so much because he had so much freedom.

"Everything went so fast. You need to think tactically about what you need to do and Rafa's English was not the best because it was his first year. He needed to make some changes but the most important thing in the locker room was that he was the one who believed we could come back.

"All our heads were down but one thing I remember is we said we need to go out and win the second half for us, for the fans, our family and everyone who believed in us. So if we won the second half then okay, that is the way it is. And the last words, we said if we scored inside 15 minutes then maybe we could come back. But no-one believed that, really."

Jerzy Dudek

The goalkeeper name-checked one of Rafa's backroom staff as a half-time inspiration in his biography *A Big Pole in our Goal* published in 2016...

"Heading to the dressing-room, I looked towards the thousands and thousands of Liverpool supporters who had travelled all the way across Europe to watch us in the Champions League final. I thought they would kick our asses, but they were calm. They probably knew that reaching the final was the best we could do and were thinking that AC Milan was a game too far. Maybe they were just stunned!

"I was furious. Our goalkeeping coach Jose Ochotorena came over to me and started to talk: 'Keep your head up, don't worry. There is the second half!'

"Everyone was broken. And with AC Milan playing so well there was potential for it to get worse. Benitez knew he must change something. He started with Traore. 'Djimi, thank you very much, go and take a shower'. He also told [Rafa's assistant] Pako Ayestaran to go and get Didi Hamann warmed up. Didi would be coming on for Djimi. It would be our second substitution as Vladimir Smicer had been brought on during the first half when Harry Kewell got injured.

"Meanwhile, Steve Finnan was with the physios and started to complain about his right thigh: 'I've no idea how long I can play with it – maybe 20 minutes? I'll do my best'. Dave Galley, our physio, whispered into Rafa's ear that Finnan might only be able to play for another 20 minutes. Rafa immediately changed his plan.

"'Okay then. Steve, thank you for your efforts but we cannot risk you. Djimi, you're back in the game, get dressed again'. When Finnan heard that he went mad. He almost attacked Galley. 'What on earth did you say to him?' he screamed. 'Substitute me? This is the Champions League final. I want to play!' Benitez stayed firm: 'We can't risk you. The decision has been made'.

"Although we were three goals down and staring down the barrel of being humiliated, it was a funny situation for Djimi. He had to come back from the showers and start looking around the dressing-room for his socks and shorts! Finnan, meanwhile, was still angry at what had just happened.

"It was chaos. When Didi came back into the dressing-room with Pako after getting warmed up, Benitez wanted to say something about the tactics, but then we heard the ref's whistle, the signal that we had to come back out onto the pitch. 'Let me think for a moment', said Rafa. 'Carra, you play on the right of the defence, Sami in the middle and Traore on the left. Riise at left wing-back, Smicer on the right. Didi, you hold the middle where we have the most problems'.

"At that moment there was a complete silence while we took stock of the changes. Then, Alex Miller, one of Rafa's assistants, spoke up.

"'Clear your heads. Don't you dare think that this could be the worst defeat in Champions League final history! They are so confident about their lead, they think they've won. Try to use it against them! If we score in the first 10 minutes we're back in it. You'll have lots of time to score another one. Then they'll panic! You need to forget what happened in the first half'.

"To be honest, Alex came across as being desperate. I'm not sure any of us believed we could get back into the game. The lads mostly thought about not getting beaten 5-0 or 6-0. But, when I think about it now, even though we started the second half slowly, I think Alex's words subconsciously boosted us, especially after we pulled a goal back."

Jamie Carragher

The centre-half and LFC legend waited until his retirement as a player before recounting in detail what happened. Here's what he wrote in his 2013 autobiography Carra...

"In that Ataturk dressing-room Rafa Benitez cemented his place in Anfield folklore. My admiration for his handling of the situation is unlimited. Rafa's conduct rarely changed, regardless of the circumstances. His calm demeanour was never required more than now.

"Privately, he must have felt the same as us. He too couldn't have failed to think about his family, or what the people of Spain would be making of his side's battering. Here he was, still struggling with his English, trying to instruct us to achieve the impossible. Good luck, I thought to myself.

"He showed few signs of emotion as he explained his changes, but the speed with which he made a series of tactical switches showed how sharp he still was. First, he told Traore to get into the shower. That was the polite code for telling a player he's being subbed. Djibril Cisse was told he'd be coming on to play on the right side and was already getting kitted out.

"As Djimi removed his shirt, an argument was brewing

between Steve Finnan and our physio Dave Galley. Finnan had damaged a groin and Dave told Rafa he thought he should be subbed. 'Finn' was distraught and pleaded to stay on. Rafa wouldn't budge. 'We've only two subs left', he explained. 'I can't afford to make two now, and if you stay on I've lost my last sub'. Traore was told to put his kit back on.

"Then, as if struck by a moment of clarity, Benitez made an abrupt decision. 'Hamann will replace Finnan and we'll play 3-5-2', he explained, displaying an assured conviction in his voice which, temporarily at least, gave me confidence. 'Pirlo is running the game from midfield, so I want Luis and Stevie to play around him and outnumber them in the middle so he can't pass the ball'.

"The swiftness of this decision confirmed to me he may have considered this formation earlier. The same set-up had worked in Turin [against Juventus], although that had been a purely defensive strategy. Part of me was thinking: okay, 45 minutes too late, but we got there in the end. Given the circumstances, it was still a brave move.

"With both Cisse and Hamann now preparing to come on, there was only one problem. 'Rafa, I think we've 12 players out there now'. Djibril would have to wait a while longer for his introduction."

Djibril Cisse

In 2018 the French striker said on French radio station RMC Sport that the skipper had made a rousing half-time speech. Jamie Carragher subsequently tweeted that it never happened! Either way...

"Benitez comes into the dressing room, he does his coach speech, that we must not give up and that we need to score quickly. Steven gets up and asks all the coaching staff to leave the dressing-room, because he wanted to be alone with just the players. All the staff left, even the physios who were giving treatment to the players.

"Stevie gets up and says that Liverpool is all he has, it is his club, all he has ever known and he does not want to be the laughing stock of the history of the Champions League. He says that if we respect him and love him as a captain, then we need to dust ourselves off and get back in the match.

"He scores the first goal, he gets the penalty. He has an extraordinary second half, finishing the game as a right-back. He has a crazy match – but that half-time speech will remain imprinted in my mind forever."

Steven Gerrard

Two years ago the Reds legend, who kickstarted the second-half comeback with his header, shared his memories on LFCTV's Retro Review Show: Istanbul 2005...

"[My memory] is wanting to talk, wanting to jump in early, wanting to say my piece early but having respect for Rafa to let him have his moment. There was a lot of commotion over an injury and the change that we needed to make, but it was very important to respect Rafa – that was his stage – and obviously let him have the first go. But I was itching to get a few things off my chest.

"There's a part in [you] that is saying it's over. But there's also a part where you think: let's reset, let's try to get an early goal, let's try to give the fans something – a bit of pride, a bit of belief – and let's not make it embarrassing. Because on the first-half showing we could have been five or six down at half-time for sure.

"We knew Rafa wanted that big moment to get a bit of belief and confidence. Without a doubt we needed the lift – we were on the floor, we thought it was over. So scoring that first early goal was a big moment."

LIVERPOOL FC
CHAMPIONS OF EUROPE
Istanbul
2005
it's ours to keep!

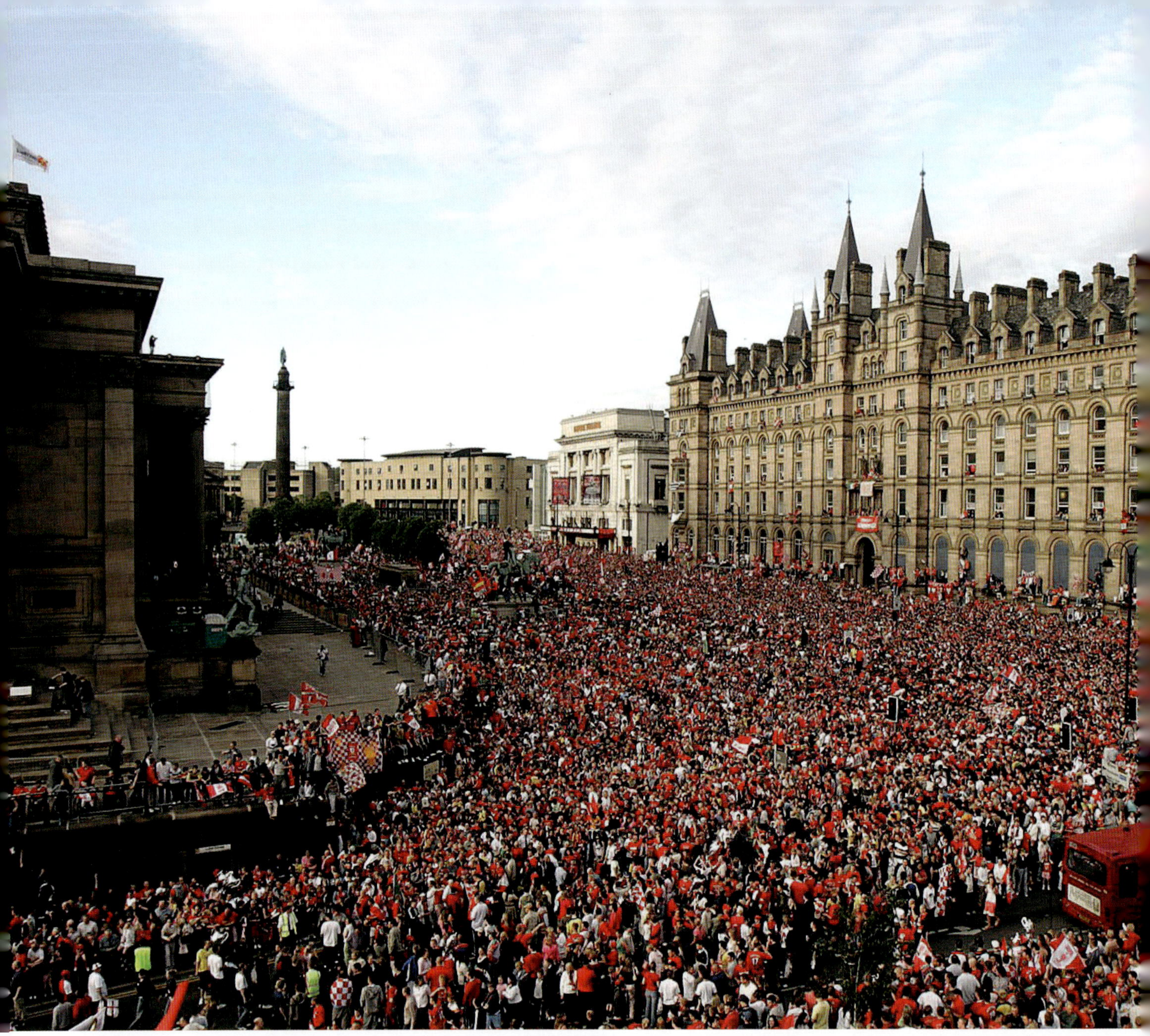

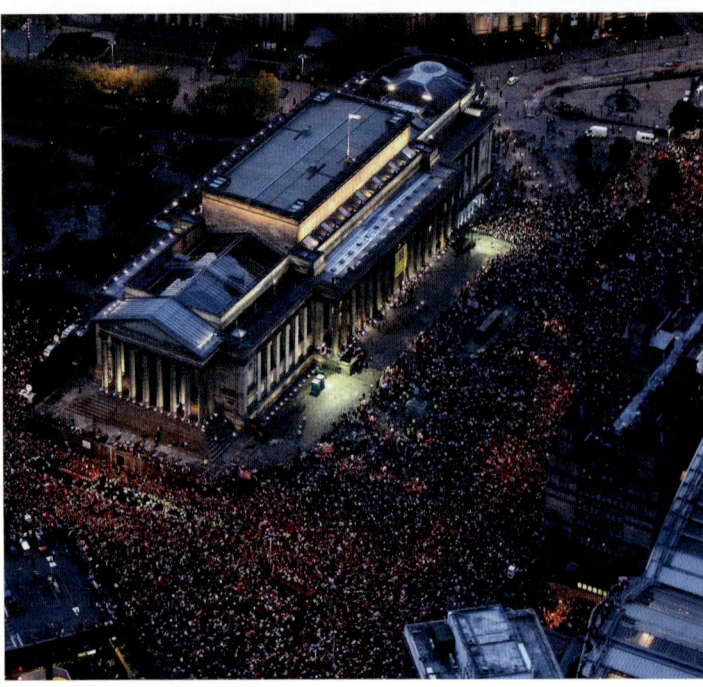

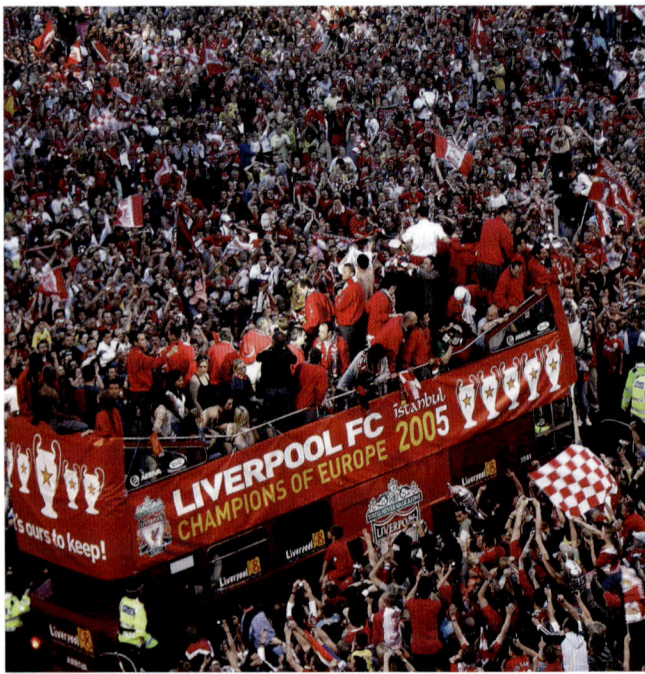

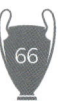

THE HOMECOMING OF ALL HOMECOMINGS

The day after the night before was one to cherish as Liverpool returned triumphant from the Champions League final in Istanbul. A sea of red and white engulfed the city as up to one million ecstatic fans lined the streets along the homecoming parade to catch a glimpse of their heroes

t had been 21 years in waiting and there was no way up to a million ecstatic Liverpool fans were going to miss the chance to greet the players who had etched their name into the club's illustrious history.

It took over four hours for the parade to make a six-mile journey from the M62 to the city centre due to the sheer volume of people who took to the streets with their banners, flags and scarves.

Up to 300,000 fans gathered outside St George's Hall for a glimpse of our legends as the city came to a standstill.

The eruption of noise and colour on their arrival was met with scenes of celebration from the players who took it in turns to show off the European Cup.

Lifting the European Cup as captain of the club he has supported all of his life was a truly proud moment for Steven Gerrard.

Bringing the trophy back to his home city saw him realise a childhood dream.

He knew it would be special but even Gerrard was taken aback by the scenes that greeted him and his team-mates as they toured the city for the biggest homecoming parade we have ever witnessed.

"It was unbelievable," he said.

"None of the players imagined there would be so many people there, waiting to cheer us on.

"The scenes were incredible. I was sitting on the plane coming home with my medal and thinking 'life can't get any better than this,' and then you saw those fans everywhere.

"Someone told me there were about a million people on the route and it was just so special.

"I can remember the celebrations following the cup treble in 2001, but this was something else. The lads were just buzzing.

"For some of the foreign players it was a real eye-opener but this is Liverpool Football Club, and that's why we never gave in against Milan when it looked like a lost cause.

"The fans in Istanbul were brilliant and the welcome home topped off the greatest night of my life. I'd just like to say thank you to everyone who turned out on behalf of all the players. Those supporters are the best."

No sleep till Hagia Sofia

Every Liverpool supporter will have their own stories of Istanbul. Here is **Stephanie Jones's** eastern European odyssey

I felt hot and queasy and my head was thumping now. The hangover had well and truly kicked in and lunch (hair-of-the-dog Efes beer included) had done little to stem it. The four of us – me, John, Bernie and Dave – were standing in the living-room-like entrance to the hotel in Istanbul's Sultanahmet district with the owner and Ahmed, the multi-lingual German 'help', talking numbers.

Turkish lira were out – we didn't have enough, nor dollars and euros – so it would have to be pounds sterling. As I had

only five, I left the fray and sat down to stare at the newspapers for the hundredth time.

Ten minutes later we were climbing into a minivan. Bernie was the first to see the cosh under the driver's seat but we all got the whiff of animal at the same time. "We'll be okay," I reassured her, not knowing if I believed it.

We pulled away to waves and goodbyes, but within 20-yards these had turned to frantic signals for us to stop.

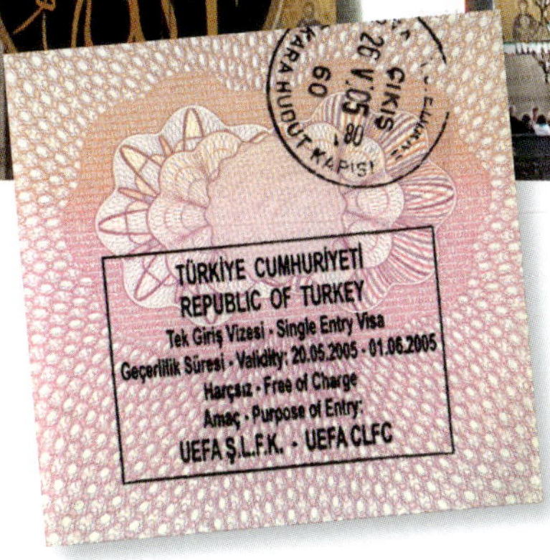

Ahmed, it appeared, was coming with us. While he ran back into the hotel, I got out to buy bottles of water and ice-lollies, and Dave got out for a cigarette. After an Anglo-Turkish confab between the hotel lady, her friend the van driver, and Ahmed, we gleaned that he (Ahmed) was going to take over the driving at the end and take us over the border into Bulgaria where we'd had to leave our hire car.

Ready to go again, I climbed back into the van. Ahmed climbed into the front and slid the door shut. "Open it! Just open it!" I turned to see the colour drain from Dave's face, his fingers trapped in the sliding door. The shop owner gave him ice, a bandage and alcohol. I gave him painkillers and Bernie bound his fingers. We pulled away and began the first leg of our long journey home...

Two days earlier I'd arrived at Heathrow a little after the others and ended up sitting next to a man from Anfield via Los Angeles on the flight. Three-and-a-half hours later we touched down in the Bulgarian capital, Sofia. There were Reds everywhere, organising lifts and taxis and minibuses, picking up their hire cars, us included. With our heads on swivels we

took down numbers and picked up leaflets in the hope of finalising the next leg or two of the journey, while John picked up the wheels. We had a pocketful of currency and two-thirds of a plan: drive from Sofia to the border with Turkey; get to Istanbul in time to see the match. From the border to the Bosporus was still hazy.

We could, of course, have flown directly to the Turkish capital, but the high-ticket prices made it a non-starter. And besides, long circuitous routes are something of a tradition for travelling Reds. Other friends had set off days before for week-long deals in Burgas and Varga on the Black Sea and Bodrum in the north of Turkey.

Initially there was talk of a ferry, but we settled on a car and booked it. That's when the rumours about not being allowed to take it over the border were found to be true.

The road from Sofia was a mess in places, but the drive was a breeze. We stopped after about 40 minutes at a roadside shop for beers, where a man squeezed into a Real Madrid shirt served us. A couple of hours later as the border came into view so too did a sign – the only one not in Cyrillic that didn't say 'bank' or 'money'. Instead: 'Morris English bar'.

"It's all falling into place," I said. "We'll park up here, ask them to call a taxi and have a beer while we're waiting." And apart from non-comprehension, misunderstanding, haggling and a lavatory straight out of Trainspotting, that's pretty much how it went. But there was nothing English about the Morris Bar, and Bulgarian beer is strong on top of Champions League final dementia. So instead of opting for the $200 taxi-ride straight to Istanbul, we went for the $80 cab option to Edirne bus station, 15km over the border.

"LUIS GAR-CIA, HE DRINKS SAN-GRIA!"

It was a mate, Dan, on the phone shouting to be heard over raucous singing, urging us to get there. He'd been bused into the capital earlier in the day, while another pal Jim and

"THERE WERE REDS EVERYWHERE ORGANISING LIFTS, TAXIS AND MINI-BUSES TO TURKEY"

his group had flown down from Bodrum. A couple of hours should do it. We piled into the Nissan Bluebird and our driver negotiated the first couple of border checkpoints. At the third we had to get out and hand over our match tickets. We were required to surrender our passports too – not quite so traumatic as having a ticket meant we didn't have to have a visa.

The remainder of the ride brought new meaning to the term 'off-roading' and I was mightily relieved to see the dim lights of the bus station even if it did resemble the end-of-the-world scene from Apocalypse Now. We knew then we should've gone all the way in the taxi, but too late. Anyway, these buses bomb through to Istanbul. So we bought the tickets, bagged the back seats, were loaded with bug repellent by the bus attendant and promptly fell asleep. We must have taken a slow one.

Our second taxi driver of the trip eventually found our hotel at 3.30 in the morning – an hour shy of 24 hours on the road. And that's when we first met Ahmed. Our rooms weren't quite ready and from the taxi we'd spied chairs on a pavement and lights in the parallel street. On further investigation it was a hotel with a bar, and it was open. We sat outside as coachloads of Milan fans showed up and it dawned on us that we were here for the final.

I remember every detail of the following day. Sitting on the roof terrace of the hotel in the morning watching Reds wander out on to balconies adjusting their scarves, pinning my Liver Bird badge on my chest, wandering up by the Blue Mosque where Milan's Rossoneri were gathered. Lunch, a taxi to the Golden Horn and the walk to Taksim Square – a jaw-dropping vision of red.

Beers and hugs – the phonecalls and texts about meeting had started hours ago – songs, banners, kickabouts and quick

checks that tickets were still in pockets. A swift dart into the Hyatt Hotel to use their facilities and see how the other half travel. Singing on the bus in the exodus from the city to the stadium, a red convoy cheered by locals lining the street.

Then abandoning the buses, now gridlocked, to hike over the waste ground with the Ataturk lit up ahead like a huge mother ship. Singer Pete Wylie's adaptation of his old hit Story Of The Blues to Story Of Emlyn Hughes, cans of Efes we'd brought with us and the never-ending stream of Reds coming up the hill, and coming, and coming, as the sun went down. Then it was time to go in.

I missed Maldini's goal. Sami missed a header. The rest of the first half is a blur – I lied when I said I remember every detail. At half-time I slumped to my seat and sat with my head in my hands imagining arriving home, going to work, meeting people, the jibes about having lost. They were the same scenarios I'd dared to imagine having won. I winced at how we'd be slaughtered by the press; at how positive I'd been (though only dared ever whisper it) that we'd win.

Then it started. The singing. You'll Never Walk Alone. I stood and joined in and the score didn't matter quite so much. We had showed we were in it together and if we didn't have hope, how could we hope the players would? Then a chant, 'We're gonna win 4-3!' I laughed at that, no one believed it of course.

Vladi's goal did it for me, that's when I believed. And as the clock ticked on I knew we'd win on penalties if it came to it. I

watched on the giant screen behind me, behind the goal, when Stevie lifted the cup. I'll remember the smile on his face forever, the way he stood in front of us joining in 'De-de-re-de-re-de-de- derrr!' to the tune of Ring Of Fire, our battle-cry of the season, and how he held up the trophy, pointing first at it then at us.

On the bus heading back to town to start the celebrations. An hour later it was back to the future as we ground to a halt, gridlocked again. We saw Maradona go past in an official-looking car then the horns and klaxons and noise kicked in. As the Turks joined in the cheers, it seemed like the whole of Istanbul was Scouse. Groups stationed themselves in and outside of bars, hanging flags, going through the repertoire of our songs. We settled outside a tiny bar in a tiny street just off Taksim Square, lapping up beers and kebabs.

"Hey queen – have ya got yer lippy with ya?" Bernie looked slightly scared. "Just write two-oh- oh-five on that." A grey-haired man pulled out a greying white flag that had four other dates scrawled on it: 1977, 1978, 1981 and 1984.

He regaled us with tales of past trips – "Ever been to Japan, when the weather's too bad to land and you're circling over the pitch with the game going on?" – his grandsons hanging on his every word. He bought a Champions League-winners shirt from a local entrepreneur and doled out cigs to passers-by – "I wouldn't see me werst enemy go without a ciggie" – before his son led him away. "Wait till me mother sees the state of you."

We said goodbye to yet more friends, Shaun and Steve, as they left to get an early- morning flight back up north, and for the second night running I heard the muezzin call-to-prayer. This time in tandem with You'll Never Walk Alone.

"I'D LEFT MY LUCKY SCARF IN LIVERPOOL – THE ONE I'D WORN TO ALL THE EUROPEAN GAMES THAT SEASON"

After what seemed like no sleep at all we wandered around the Hagia Sofia, the stunning Byzantine basilica, where kids shook our hands and told us we were champions, before adjourning for refreshment. And it was there that we decided to ditch the idea of a bus back to the Bulgarian border in favour of a taxi instead. I set off to start negotiations.

We slept most of the way back to Bulgaria and the cosh remained under the seat. When we reached the border our makeshift cabbie parked up and we discovered Ahmed wasn't going to drive us over at all – he'd come along to cross it with us in order to get another visa himself – so we were all walking. A guard waved us through. "Liverpool – champions!" he beamed. He was right.

We passed the fourth checkpoint, past the rows of waiting cars and stepped back into Bulgaria. Ahmed got his visa; we got back to the Morris Bar and our hire car. We drove back to Sofia where we found a hotel for the night before flying home. Easy.

Yes, there had been hitches. Ten minutes after arriving in Istanbul in the small hours our taxi had skidded to avoid a jack-knifing lorry that smashed into the too-low ceiling of an underpass, small boulders of concrete bouncing off our cab's roof and windscreen.

I was mugged in another taxi, the driver leaning over to snatch money from my purse, and I'd left my scarf in Liverpool – my lucky European scarf that I'd worn to all our continental games that season, the one I'd had since my dad took me to my first European final, the UEFA Cup at Anfield in 1973.

But none of it mattered now. We were champions of Europe for the fifth time. And Dave's fingers were on the mend.

ALL TOGETHER!

*There were **27** men who featured along the way as Liverpool FC lifted their fifth European Cup. Here's a look at all those who played a part on the pitch...*

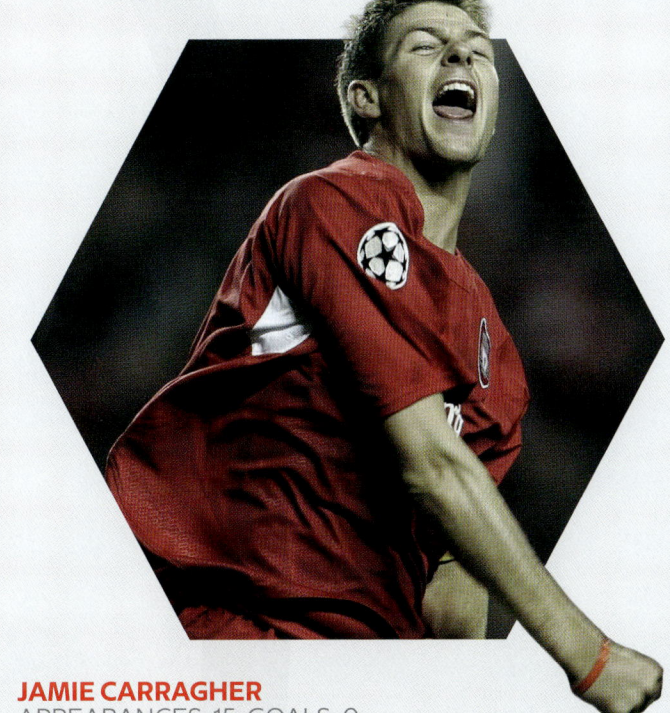

STEVEN GERRARD
APPEARANCES: 10. GOALS: 4.

Liverpool's captain fantastic whose header started the incredible fightback in Istanbul.

His wonder strike against Olympiakos had also saved the Reds from early elimination in the final group game.

As a local lad, the sense of pride was obvious as he followed in the footsteps of legendary Liverpool leaders Emlyn Hughes, Phil Thompson and Graeme Souness to lift the European Cup.

Gerrard played 10 games in the Reds' triumphant campaign and also scored both goals in the game that started the run to glory in Rafa Benitez's first competitive match in charge – the 2-0 win at Grazer AK in the qualifier.

JAMIE CARRAGHER
APPEARANCES: 15. GOALS: 0.

Liverpool's Lionheart gave some stupendous displays at centre-back and full-back as the Reds won 'Ol Big Ears' for the fifth time.

He produced heroics in the final against AC Milan and put his body on the line time after time to help Liverpool to one of the club's proudest days.

Carragher was one of only three players to appear in all 15 games on the Reds' road to the triumph, from the opening qualifier against Grazer AK through to the highs and lows of Istanbul.

His efforts were recognised by a fan banner of a similar style to that made by supporters in the 1970s in honour of another all-action European Cup hero, Joey Jones.

SAMI HYYPIA
APPEARANCES: 15. GOALS: 1.

Another ever-present on Liverpool's path to glory, the big Finn was at the heart of some epic defensive displays in the latter stages.

His commanding displays and willingness to put his body on the line came to the fore in the goalless draw against Juventus in the Stadio Dell'Alpi and the first leg stalemate against Chelsea in the semi-final at Stamford Bridge.

He also produced a stunning goal in the Anfield encounter with Juve, opening the scoring in the quarter final after only 10 minutes with a well-taken finish at the Anfield Road end.

His contributions were recognised by Liverpudlians who regularly sang 'Oh Sami, Sami...' in acclamation.

JOHN ARNE RIISE
APPEARANCES: 15. GOALS: 1.

The Norwegian was one of three Reds who figured in every game along the way to the club's fifth European Cup triumph.

The left-sided fans' favourite produced typically all-action displays both at full-back and, at times, in a more advanced position.

He fired a powerful low free-kick past goalkeeper Jörg Butt to put the Reds two goals to the good in the first leg of the last 16 clash with Bayer Leverkusen at Anfield.

Although he may have missed in the penalty shoot-out in Istanbul, he had earlier supplied the assist from which Steven Gerrard headed Liverpool back into the game against AC Milan.

STEVE FINNAN
APPEARANCES: 14. GOALS: 0.

Known for his consistency of performance, he played in all but one of the Reds' 15 fixtures.

The right-back was famously substituted at half-time of the final against AC Milan in Istanbul after sustaining a thigh strain in the first half. Physio Dave Galley informed Rafa Benitez that the Republic of Ireland defender needed to be replaced and so Didi Hamann came on in his place.

"I always say I changed the game that night," Finnan told the Liverpool Echo in 2015.

"If I hadn't have got injured, we wouldn't have won the European Cup. That injury I got was the best thing that ever happened to Liverpool."

MILAN BAROS
APPEARANCES: 14. GOALS: 2.

The lively Czech forward was another who played in all but one of the Reds matches en route to ultimate victory.

The pacy no5 came off the bench to wrap things up with Liverpool's second of the night in the group stage game against Monaco at Anfield and almost six months later scored the Reds' third goal in the round of 16 second leg at Bayer Leverkusen to help tee up a quarter-final with Juventus.

Baros started the final in Istanbul and was replaced by Djibril Cisse five minutes before the end of normal time.

LUIS GARCIA
APPEARANCES: 12. GOALS: 5.

Five foot seven of football heaven, the Spaniard scored some vital goals along the way.

The club's top scorer in Europe that season, his brilliant volley in the home leg of the quarter-final against Juventus was probably the best but his semi-final strike, dubbed a 'ghost goal' by fans of the Blues, was undoubtedly the most important.

Garcia's debut season with the Reds also saw him score three times against Bayer Leverkusen in the round of 16, once in the first leg at Anfield as Liverpool built a 3-1 lead and twice more in the Bay Arena as the Reds repeated the scoreline in Germany.

HARRY KEWELL
APPEARANCES: 12. GOALS: 0.

In many ways, the final against AC Milan seemed to sum up the Australian's career at Liverpool.

Named in Rafael Benitez's starting line-up, the winger lasted only 23 minutes before having to limp out through injury with Vladimir Smicer coming on as his replacement.

Despite his injury record, Kewell figured in a dozen of the 15 games in the Reds' triumphant run.

Among his important contributions were the assist for Florent Sinama-Pongolle's equaliser in the crucial group game against Olympiakos which helped provide the catalyst for the Reds' storming second-half fightback.

DIETMAR HAMANN
APPEARANCES: 10. GOALS: 1.

Didi's introduction as a half-time substitute in Istanbul proved crucial.

During the first half, the Brazilian midfielder Kaka had exploited the space afforded to him as AC Milan dominated the first-half.

However, an injury to Steve Finnan saw Rafael Benitez re-shape his team during the interval at the Ataturk Stadium and Liverpool didn't look back.

'Der Kaiser' played in 10 games as the Reds lifted European football's biggest club prize and the defensive midfielder also scored with a late free-kick in the round of 16 first leg against Bayer Leverkusen at Anfield to give his team a 3-1 advantage to take into the return fixture in his homeland.

DJIMI TRAORE
APPEARANCES: 10. GOALS: 0.

One of Liverpool's unsung heroes of 2004/05, the defender played all 120 minutes of the final against AC Milan in Istanbul.

After the Reds had fought their way back to parity from trailing 3-0 at the break, he made a vital goalline clearance to deny Andriy Shevchenko a winning goal.

Rafael Benitez had utilised the Frenchman's versatility throughout the tournament, deploying him either at centre-back or at left-back and he always gave his best for the cause.

He was into his sixth full season with Liverpool and performed admirably, starting both legs of the quarter-final against Juventus and semi-final against Chelsea.

JERZY DUDEK
APPEARANCES: 10. GOALS:0.

The Reds' no1, the 'big Pole in our goal' made some gravity-defying saves towards the end of extra-time in the final against AC Milan, then excelled in the penalty shoot-out to secure victory for Liverpool.

His double save from Andriy Shevchenko still beggars belief watching it back a couple of decades on, while he later made saves from Andra Pirlo and Shevchenko in the shoot-out to ensure that the famous trophy returned to Anfield.

Jerzy featured in 10 of the games along the road to glory and was one of three goalkeepers used by Rafael Benitez, alongside Chris Kirkland and Scott Carson.

DJIBRIL CISSE
APPEARANCES: 9. GOALS: 1.

Cisse had famously agreed to join Liverpool from Auxerre to link up with compatriot Gerard Houllier at Anfield.

The French manager parted company with Liverpool before that could happen but Rafael Benitez happily embraced the striker in his first Reds squad.

Injury restricted his availability but he always offered an attacking threat and scored the Reds' first goal of the group stage, opening the scoring in the 2-0 home defeat of Monaco.

He replaced Milan Baros towards the end of normal time in the final in Istanbul and stepped forward to take the Reds' second kick of the penalties, beating AC Milan goalkeeper Dida to put Liverpool 2-0 up in the shoot-out.

IGOR BISCAN
APPEARANCES: 9. GOALS: 0

The Anfield cult hero solidified his status amongst supporters by playing an important role in the Reds' run to Istanbul.

Despite having been informed by Rafael Benitez that he was free to find a new club upon the expiry of his contract at the end of the season, the Croatian still gave his all and produced some of his best performances.

He revelled in deputising for Steven Gerrard in the group stage game at Deportivo La Coruna.

Igor also played from the start against Bayer Leverkusen in the last 16, Juventus in the quarter-finals and in the semi-finals against Chelsea but remained on the bench for the final.

XABI ALONSO
APPEARANCES: 8. GOALS: 1

The gifted playmaker had settled in quickly at Anfield and soon earned legendary status with his goal in the final.

After seeing his spot kick saved by AC Milan goalkeeper Dida, he reacted quickly to convert the rebound and complete Liverpool's incredible six-minute comeback.

The Basque native had suffered a broken ankle in the 2005 New Year's Day clash against Chelsea but returned three months later to feature in the second leg of the quarter-final with Juventus as the Reds drew 0-0 in Turin. He suffered more misfortune against Chelsea when his harsh yellow card in the 0-0 semi-final first leg draw at Stamford Bridge saw him banned for the return, but Liverpool saw off Jose Mourinho's men in his absence.

JOSEMI
APPEARANCES: 7. GOALS: 0.

With Markus Babbel moving on at the end of the 2003/04 season, Liverpool needed a new right-back in their squad.

Rafael Benitez brought in Malaga's Josemi Rey with the minimum of fuss, making his Spanish compatriot his first signing for a reported fee of around £2 million.

With Jamie Carragher often deployed as a full-back, Josemi was by no means a regular but he still played in seven of the games on the road to Liverpool's fifth European Cup triumph and made five starts and two sub appearances in the qualifying and knockout stages.

He was an unused substitute in Istanbul.

VLADIMIR SMICER
APPEARANCES: 6. GOALS: 1.

What better way to end your Liverpool career than with a goal in a European Cup final and the conversion of what proved to be the winning penalty?

Vladi started the night in Turkey unsure whether he would add to his 183 appearances for the club having been named among the substitutes.

But an injury to Harry Kewell saw him summoned to join the action after just 23 minutes and he quickly came to the fore.

His long-range strike brought the arrears to 3-2 and he successfully slotted home Liverpool's fourth penalty of the shoot-out which gave them a 3-2 spot-kick triumph when Andriy Shevchenko was denied by Jerzy Dudek moments later.

STEPHEN WARNOCK
APPEARANCES: 6. GOALS: 0.

The Ormskirk-born left-back enjoyed a breakthrough season under Rafael Benitez, making 30 appearances which included half a dozen in Europe.

After coming through the Reds' Academy, he was handed his senior debut in Rafael Benitez's first game in charge, coming off the bench to replace Steven Gerrard for the final 10 minutes of the qualifying win at Grazer AK.

He was given two starts in the competition – the group game at Olympiakos and the second leg of the round of 16 tie at Bayer Leverkusen, and gave a good account of himself as he established himself as an important part of Benitez's first Liverpool squad.

ANTONIO NUNEZ
APPEARANCES: 5. GOALS: 0.

The winger joined the Reds ahead of the summer transfer deadline as part of the deal which took Michael Owen to Real Madrid.

Nicknamed 'Tony' by supporters, he soon became something of a cult figure at Anfield and fans were pictured with a cardboard cutout of him before the first leg of the semi-final against Chelsea at Stamford Bridge.

In what was his only season with the Reds, Nunez featured in important games, figuring in both legs of the quarter-final against Juventus and coming off the subs' bench in the second leg of the semi-final victory over Chelsea in L4.

He was among the unused subs in Istanbul.

FLORENT SINAMA-PONGOLLE
APPEARANCES: 4. GOALS: 1.

The French forward scored a vitally important goal at a time when it looked like the Reds' European run would end before Christmas.

When Rivaldo scored for Olympiakos 26 minutes into Liverpool's final game of the group stage, the Reds went in at half-time knowing they would need to win by two clear goals.

Rafael Benitez brought on Flo for defender Djimi Traore and the effect was almost immediate.

Just two minutes later, Harry Kewell worked some magic down the left and picked out Flo's run to the near post. He tapped in at the Kop end to start a second-half three-goal fightback. Sound familiar?

CHRIS KIRKLAND
APPEARANCES: 4. GOALS: 0.

The keeper was into his fourth and final season at Anfield and played his part in helping the Reds win European Cup number five.

He started four of the 15 games that season, starting with back-to-back clean sheets in the group stage double-header against Deportivo La Coruna. Kirkland was also named in goal for the 1-0 defeat at Monaco before taking his place between the sticks on that epic Anfield night against Olympiakos.

Despite performing well, Rafael Benitez's decision to sign another young keeper in Scott Carson in January 2005 effectively brought the curtain down on Kirkland's Anfield career.

SALIF DIAO
APPEARANCES: 3. GOALS: 0.

The Senegalese midfielder was a bit-part player throughout the 2004/05 campaign, making only 14 appearances.

Three of those came in Europe with the former Sedan man featuring before Christmas.

He came on as a sub for Milan Baros with 18 minutes remaining of Rafael Benitez's first game in charge, the 2-0 win at Grazer AK in the qualifying round. He then started the return leg against the Austrians at Anfield.

His only other outing in the Champions League that season came as a late substitute for Dietmar Hamann in the group stage defeat at Olympiakos.

DARREN POTTER
APPEARANCES: 3. GOALS: 0.

The Liverpudlian was one of a number of young players handed opportunities by Rafael Benitez in the Spaniard's first season in charge.

He was usually deployed in a wide position and made three appearances in Europe, expressing his delight at opportunities for first-team football.

"I am more comfortable in the middle than on the right, but you know that Steven Gerrard, the best player in Europe, Xabi Alonso and Didi Hamann are competing for those places, so it is not going to be easy playing there. But as far as I am concerned, I'd give an arm and a leg just to get a shirt in any position."

ANTHONY LE TALLEC
APPEARANCES: 3. GOALS: 0.

The talented Frenchman only appeared seven times during the 2004/05 season with three of those outings coming in Europe.

His first appearance of the season came as a second-half substitute for Harry Kewell in the 3-1 win over Bayer Leverkusen at Anfield in the round of 16 first leg.

Rafael Benitez showed his faith in Le Tallec when he handed him a start in the home quarter-final first leg against Juventus and the no13 provided the assist for Luis Garcia's wonder-strike at the Anfield Road end that put Liverpool two goals to the good inside 25 minutes.

He then replaced Garcia as a late sub a week later in Italy as the Reds booked their place in the semi-finals by seeing out a 0-0 draw in the Stadio Dell Alpi.

NEIL MELLOR
APPEARANCES: 2. GOALS: 1.

The young striker was another to be given chances by Rafael Benitez and he didn't disappoint.

Just over a week after his dramatic late Kop end winner against Arsenal in the Premier League, Mellor was at it again in the crucial must-win game against Olympiakos.

Liverpool trailed 1-0 at the break and needed to win by two clear goals.

Florent Sinama-Pongolle had made it 1-1 on the night before he pounced with 10 minutes remaining to put the Reds 2-1 up.

Then, with four minutes left on the clock, he teed up Steven Gerrard for the captain's dramatic thunderbolt that sealed a 3-1 victory and progression to the knockout stages.

SCOTT CARSON
APPEARANCES: 1. GOALS: 0.

Signed as a teenager from Leeds United for a reported £1 million in January 2005, Carson was one of three players to make a single appearance as the Reds claimed the European Cup.

The Whitehaven-born goalkeeper was thrown in at the deep end when he started the home quarter-final against Juventus, but he proved up to the task.

He was beaten by a Fabio Cannavaro header but also made some important saves as the Reds secured a 2-1 first leg advantage to take to Turin.

Carson's whirlwind season ended with him taking a place on the substitutes' bench as the Reds completed their dramatic comeback in Istanbul.

JOHN WELSH
APPEARANCES: 1. GOALS: 0.

The local lad made a single substitutes' appearance in Liverpool's triumphant campaign.

A midfielder who joined the club's Academy as a 10-year-old and came through the ranks, he was given his opportunity to taste Champions League football in the round of 16 tie at Bayer Leverkusen.

With Liverpool leading 3-0 on the night at Bay Arena and 6-1 on aggregate, Rafael Benitez sent Welsh on for the final 20 minutes in place of Jamie Carragher.

It was one of the highlights of his senior Liverpool career as he left the club at the end of that season, signing for Hull City in a bid to play more regular first-team football.

STEPHANE HENCHOZ
APPEARANCES: 1. GOALS: 0.

When Rafael Benítez took over in 2004/05 it became apparent that the Swiss centre-back didn't feature in his long-term plans.

Henchoz had been plagued by injury in the previous two seasons and although he had made a fine contribution to the Reds, his days at Anfield appeared numbered.

"If there's a block to be made in the area and you see a red shirt flying in to prevent a goal, you can be fairly sure it will have a no2 on the back of it," said former Reds' assistant manager Phil Thompson.

Henchoz started the 1-0 reverse at home to Grazer AK in the second leg of the qualifier but joined Celtic in January 2005.

TAKSIM FOR RAFA

Another fan's story:
James Mason's poignant
package-holiday caper

Jim today (left) with Little Joe, his cousin's son

t still makes me smile when I hear the quiz question: which UEFA Champions League winner scored twice in the same game on two different days?

The answer of course is Vladimir Smicer, the Czech pocket-rocket who followed our mighty captain's lead to put AC Milan on the back-foot with a goal around 10.45pm local time Istanbul on that miraculous Wednesday night, then dispatched his spot-kick in the shoot-out on what was technically Thursday morning.

I've kept all the text messages from that evening. Before the penalties, as I stood in the Ataturk there was one which said: Oh my God... When you see Dudek's save from Shevchenko it defies logic he had his hand out horizontal to the ground and it hit it and went over... there's no way it shouldn't of [sic] gone in ... that was a miracle! Enjoy, enjoy, enjoy, enjoy.

"IT WORKED OUT CHEAPER TO HEAD TO BODRUM FOR A HOLIDAY PACKAGE AND FLY TO ISTANBUL"

We'd been to every away game on the journey to Istanbul: from jumping in the LFC coach convoy in our hired mini-van on the way to Juventus then dodging tear-gas outside the ground; to gate-crashing a posh yacht party in Genoa (en route to Turin); having a very drunk photo taken with Igor Biscan outside the ground after the Bayer Leverkusen game; and sitting outside a Euro-bar on the F1 Grand Prix circuit in Monaco (after the group game) until the early hours topping up our £8 bottles of lager from a holdall under the table full of ale – as the baffled bar owner wondered just how we could make a single drink last so long.

As every seasoned European campaigner knows, the logistics of trying to out-do the airlines and hotels as prices rocket through the roof once the draw is announced, is all part of the fun. And Istanbul must have been a watershed moment in terms of how everyone got to Taksim Square on the morning of 25 May 2005. Bill Shankly, originator of that great quote about Chairman Mao and the show of red strength, would have been proud of this gathering from every corner of the globe.

Our group's journey started with a holiday package to the Aegean resort of Bodrum – we'd found it was cheaper to fly out there for a week's all-inclusive, get an internal flight up to Istanbul then come back for the rest of the holiday. The holiday worked out at just under £250 each and the internal flight was £99 return, and then two cheap nights in a hostel – a bargain compared with some of the prices being offered for flights alone.

What made this European trip so special was my cousin Joe bringing his son. I am two years older than Joe and way back in 1977 we'd met at Rome's Trevi fountain at 2pm on 25 May for our first European Cup final. Joe was 14 and had travelled all the way by coach from Liverpool. I'd travelled from London by train-ferry-train (by then my side of the family had moved to the capital when I was younger).

Twenty-eight years later to the day, there was Joe standing in Taksim Square with his 14-year-old lad. It was a poignant moment, more so now because two years and four months later Joe died of cancer, which is why Istanbul holds such special memories for me.

But in Bodrum beforehand, no sooner had we got to our hotel rooms and dropped off our bags than we grabbed two days' worth of clothes and it was back in a cab down to the airport to

Jim at the Ataturk with cousin Joe, Little Joe and mate Mark

grab our internal flight up to Istanbul. As we arrived at departures there were half-a-dozen other Reds with the same idea. I was with a mate from my local football team, Mark, another lifelong Red whose mum had moved from Liverpool down to London years earlier.

The taxi to Bodrum airport from our resort hotel was nowhere near as exciting as the one back – dodging lightning bolts which hit the road with a driver stumped by his new cab's window-screen de-mister. By then, though, we were European champions, and if I had a pound for every time I saw a shake of a Turkish head then heard the words "Liverpool – incredible!" in broken English, I'd be a rich man indeed.

We arrived in Istanbul the night before the game, checked into our hostel, found our beds, dumped our stuff and headed out to Taksim Square. Then me, Mark, Joe and little Joe found a bar and it was the start of an amazing two days. This was also the first time we heard the Luis Garcia song belted out by a packed bar all night as the Efes Pilsner flowed.

I know the Turkish fans have a reputation for their passion, but the mobile Kop impressed even the locals. The bar-owner said one of the leading Galatasaray ultras had been in and was impressed with the singing of the fans. And they all wanted Liverpool to win.

We must have staggered back to the hostel about 4am, but with all the excitement we were up again at nine for breakfast. Everyone in the hostel must have slept with their ticket that night! The rest of the morning was sightseeing then a few drinks and meeting up with more friends. Everyone wanted to know the words to the new Luis Garcia song. We heard of people were offering thousands of pounds for match tickets, but I am not sure there were many takers.

It was only aboard the convoy of buses to the stadium that we realized how far it was from the centre of Istanbul. But as we weaved through crowded streets and into the suburbs everyone was in full voice, as hordes of local kids ran alongside the bus chanting "Liverpool! Liverpool!" and banging on the sides.

The buses pulled up a fair way from the ground and we had to walk the rest of the way, through a barren wasteland of dirt-

"LOCAL KIDS RAN ALONGSIDE THE BUSES CHANTING 'LIVERPOOL!' AND BANGING THE SIDES"

mounds as the stadium began to take shape like some kind of mythical phoenix. As we looked back, it was like a scene from Zulu – more and more Reds coming over the hill. It's a sight that lives long in the memory. I think this would even have taken Shanks' breath away.

We took up two-thirds of the stadium that night – it was a sea of red. The choreographed mass of Milan fans were no match for the mighty travelling Kop. And our flags and banners were everywhere, the running track completely covered, every space with something tied to it, hung from it, as the acrid smell of flare smoke wafted through the air.

As I say, I've kept all the texts, from three-nil down and miserable to comeback-crazy and penalty madness. There's one from my late mum the day after that just says: 'They're saying God was a Scouser last night'.

The after-show party was long and hard. There were smiles, hugs, singsongs and tears of joy. We were back and a manager from Madrid had put us there. Two years later he got us there again, and this time we stayed on a Greek island, but that's another story.

THE NIGHT AT **THE MUSEUM**

The LFC Museum is a treasure trove detailing the Reds' rich history. The current displays include a section dedicated to objects of interest from Istanbul. Here is a look at some of the items in the club's possession which provide lasting reminders of that incredible night

01

02

03

04

"Man of the Match"
AC Milan - Liverpool FC
Atatürk Olympic Stadium
Istanbul, 25 May 2005

05

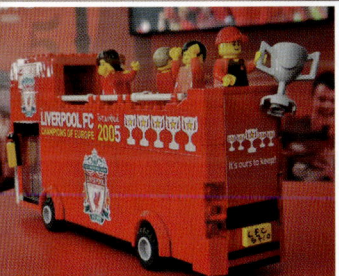

1. HATS OFF:
A red and green hat that was presented to Liverpool supporters by club sponsors Carlsberg

2. THE MATCHBALL:
A used matchball from the Champions League final, personally collected by Steven Gerrard at the end of the game

3. MOTM AWARD:
UEFA's 2005 Champions League final man of the match plaque that was later presented to Reds' captain Steven Gerrard

4. TOASTING SUCCESS:
Commemorative champagne flutes which were presented by UEFA to club directors

5. JUST THE TICKET:
An original match ticket for the Ataturk Stadium on 25 May 2005

6. LOCAL BREW:
An unopened can of Efes beer from the time, similar to those consumed by thousands of fans around Istanbul

7. READ ALL ABOUT IT:
The official matchday programme issued by UEFA for the final

8. BUILD IT UP:
Lego produced a limited edition of 500 kits of the Reds' homecoming parade bus, featuring the Liverpool FC club crest and the '5 times' emblem

9. JERZY'S JERSEY:
The match-worn shirt of inspirational Liverpool goalkeeper Jerzy Dudek

10. SPECIAL SCARF:
A commemorative matchday scarf featuring the date of the final

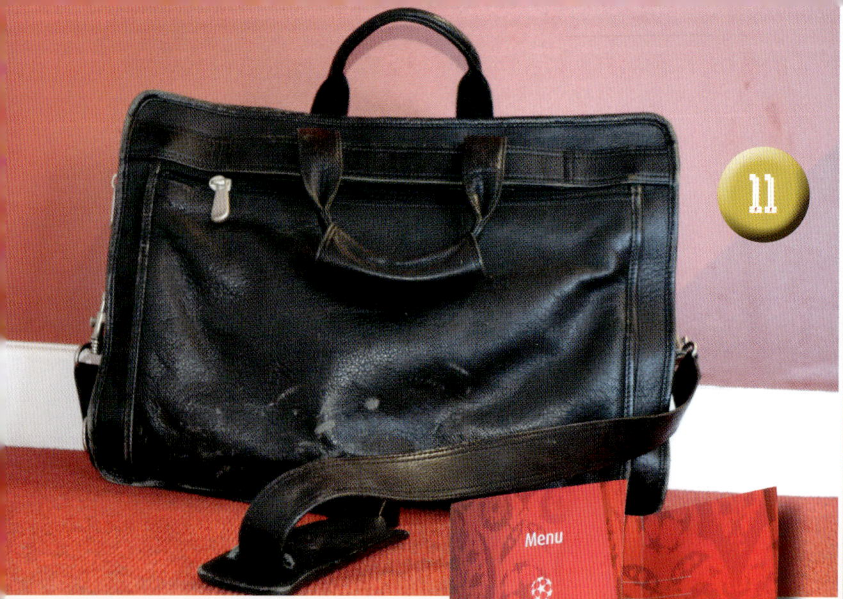

11

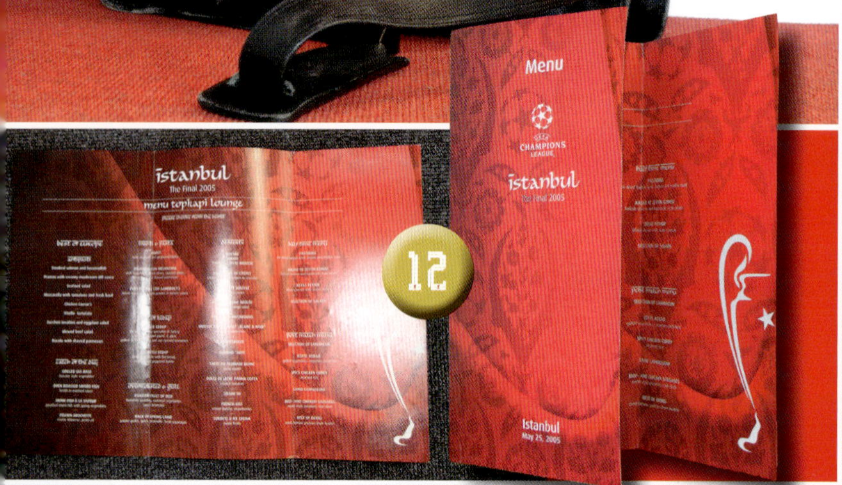

12

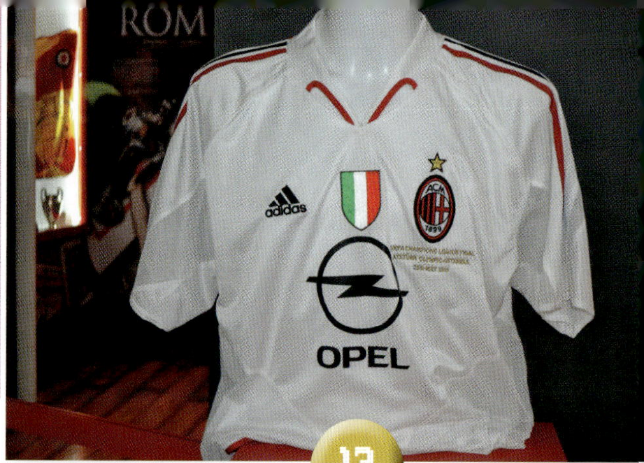

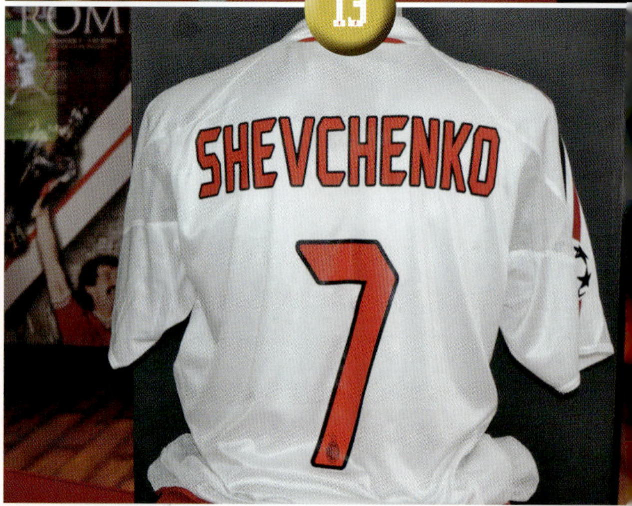

13

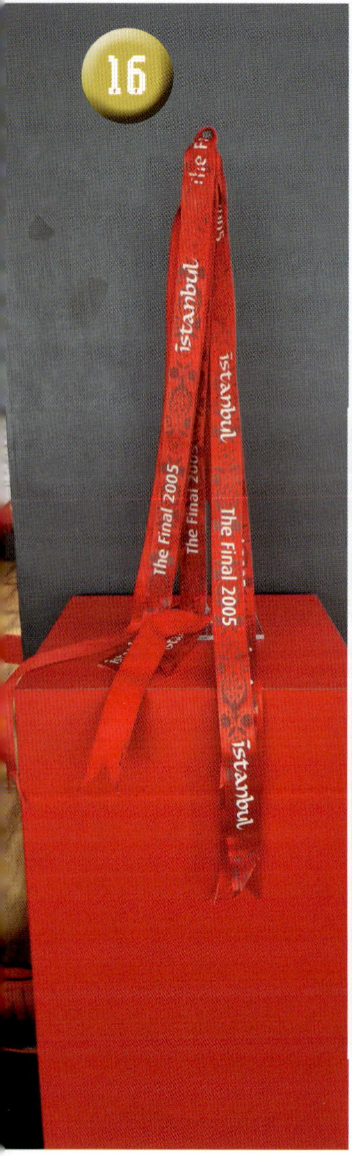

SHEVCHENKO

7

16

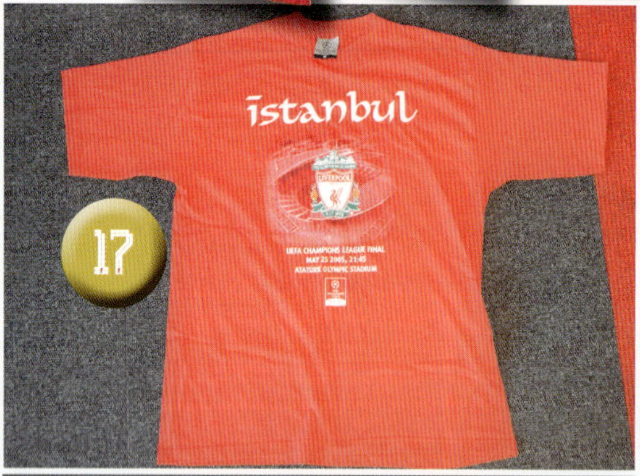

istanbul
The Final 2005
The Final 2005
The Final 2005
The Final 2005
istanbul
istanbul

17

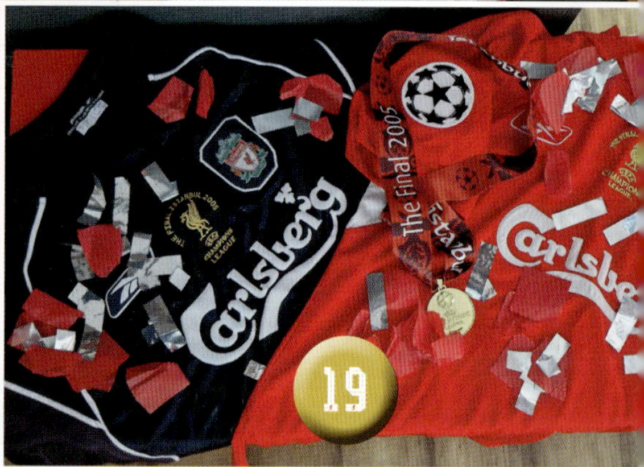

istanbul

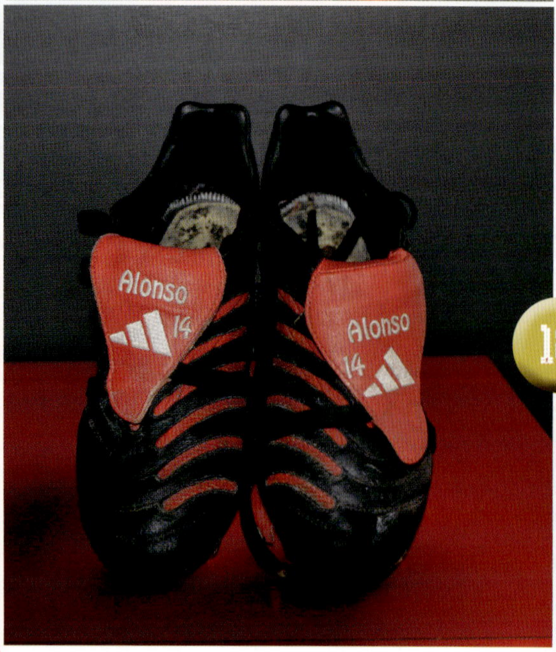

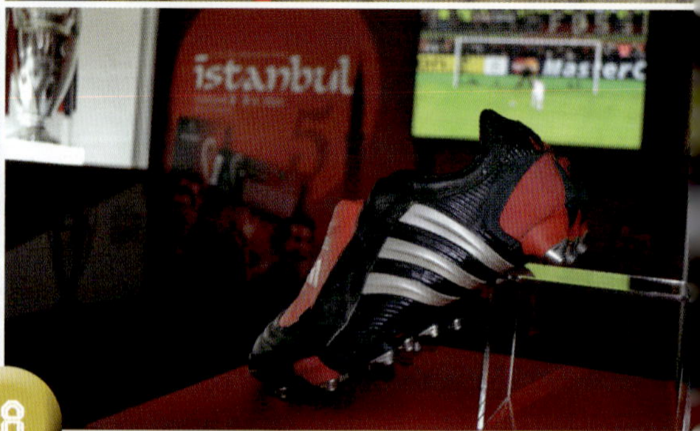

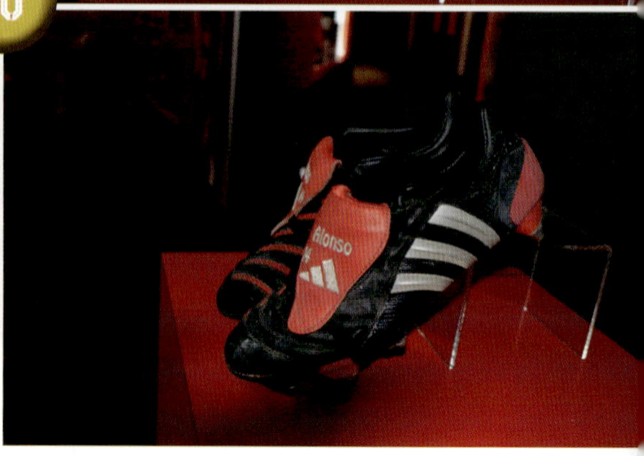

18

Alonso
14
Alonso
14

Alonso

19

Carlsberg
Carlsberg
The Final 2005

* To visit the new and improved LFC Museum,
which is included in all Tours & Experiences,
visit liverpoolfc.com/stadiumtours

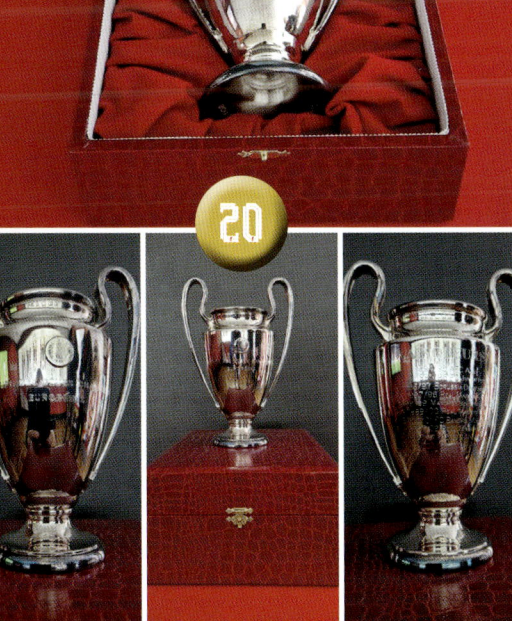

Istanbul
2005

11. RAFAS BRIEFCASE:
The original briefcase in which Liverpool manager Rafael Benitez kept his notes for the final

12. MATCHDAY MENU:
A commemorative matchday menu from one of the lounges at the Ataturk Stadium

13. SHEVA'S SHIRT:
The shirt worn in the final by AC Milan striker Andriy Shevchenko. He later gave it to Steven Gerrard

14. CAPTAIN MARVEL:
Steven Gerrard's match-worn shirt, captain's armband and winner's medal from the 2005 Champions League final

15. FIVE STAR HEROES:
A close up of the medals presented to the triumphant Reds squad by UEFA after the final whistle

16. RED RIBBONS
The ribbons that adorned the trophy which was presented to Liverpool in Istanbul

17. GOT THE T-SHIRT?:
A t-shirt celebrating the 2005 final which was a part of UEFA's official merchandise range

18. XABI'S BOOTS
The boots in which midfielder Xabi Alonso scored Liverpool's equalising goal against AC Milan in Istanbul

19. TICKER TAPE:
Some of the actual ticker-tape that was used in the post-match celebrations, displayed here on a couple of the Reds' iconic jerseys

20. LITTLE EARS!:
A miniature 2005 Champions League trophy, which was presented by UEFA to each of the Reds' winning squad

21. SUPER SKIPPER:
The captain's armband worn by Steven Gerrard on the famous night

22. OURS TO KEEP:
The trophy that the Reds were allowed to keep after winning the competition for the fifth time

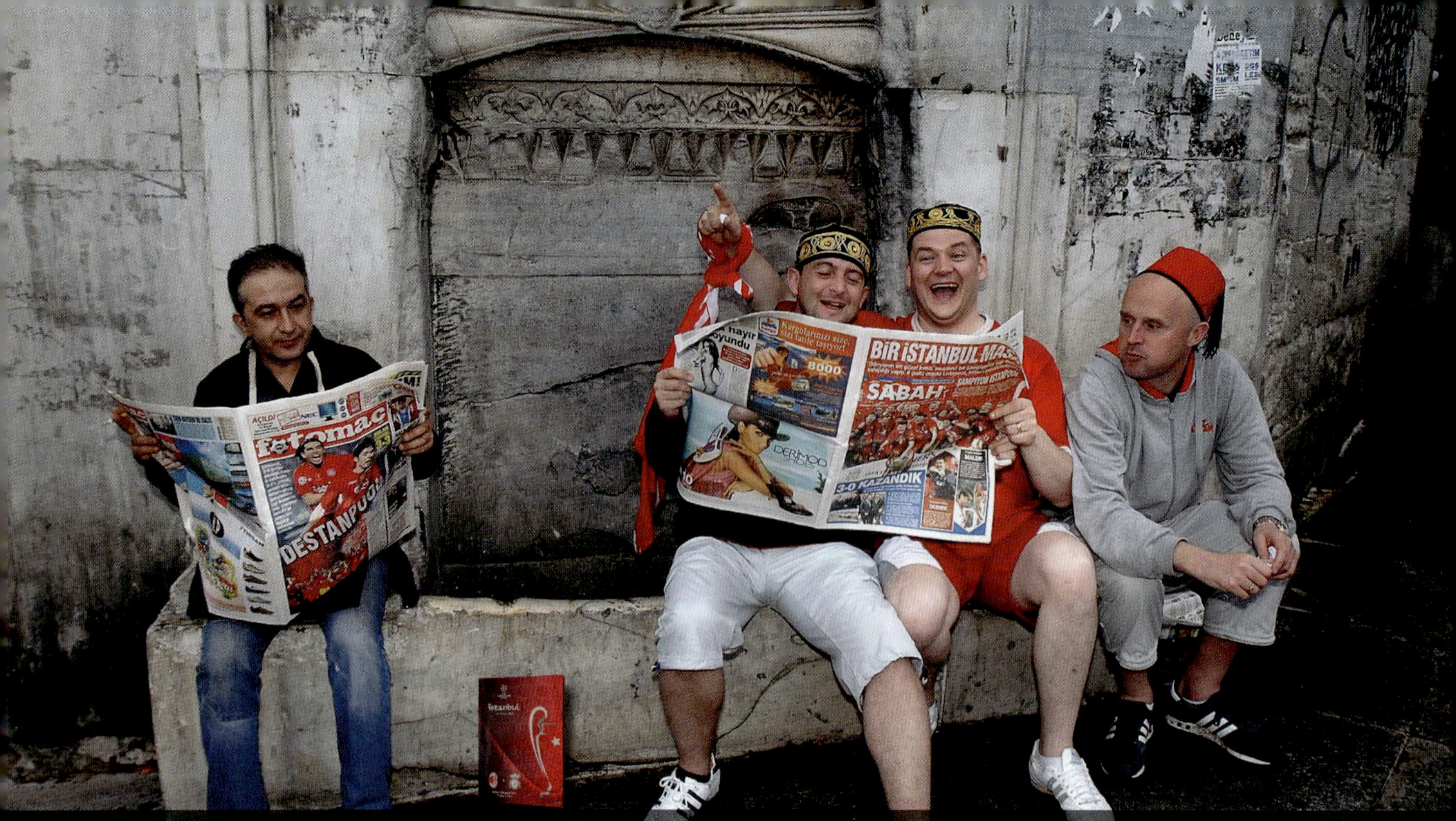

FULLY **PROGRAMMED**

__ANDY MARSDEN__, aka __LFCProgMan__, revisits the 2004/05 UEFA Champions League matchday programmes - official and unofficial - from the qualifier at Grazer to Istanbul

Pre-season in 2004 was cut short by the small matter of taking part in the Champions League. No Liverpool supporter will forget this Champions League campaign. It began at the Arnold Schwarzenegger Stadion in Graz, where they took on Grazer AK (also known as GAK) in the third qualifying round.

There was no official programme, just a black-and-white photocopied teamsheet, issued to the media. A Liverpool supporter reports being sent a batch of glossy teamsheets by a GAK official, whom he had met at the match. It is understood these were available in the media and VIP areas only and, due to limited supply, are very rare. Later in the season, an unofficial programme was available on some online auction sites. It has the look and feel of publications by Steffen Pockart, but this remains unconfirmed. During this era, he sold a number of programmes of this style for matches involving Liverpool, but never at the ground, only online. These were usually friendlies, when no official programme had been produced. Liverpool qualified for the Group Stage thanks to the aggregate score; this, despite the huge scare caused by losing 1-0 back at Anfield.

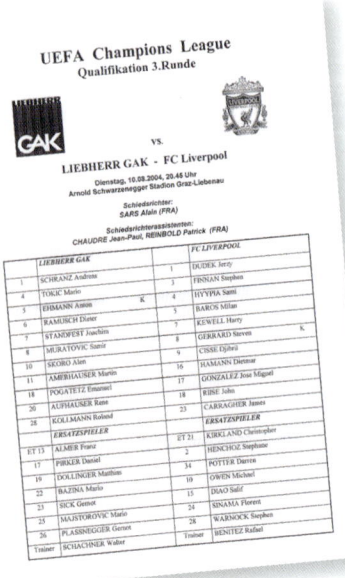

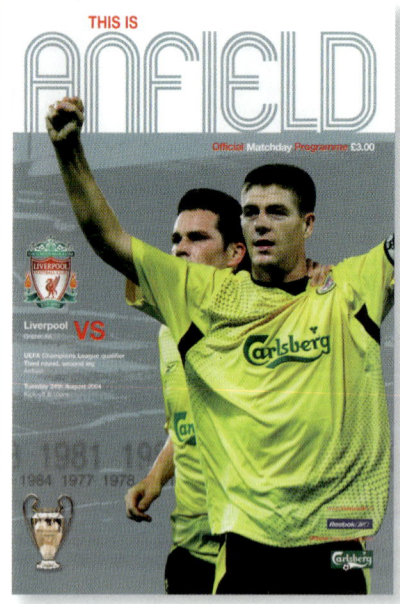

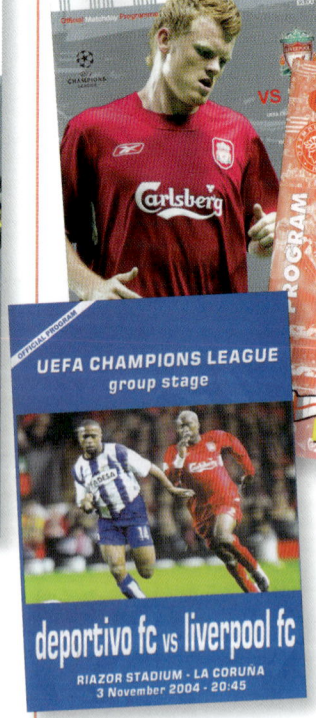

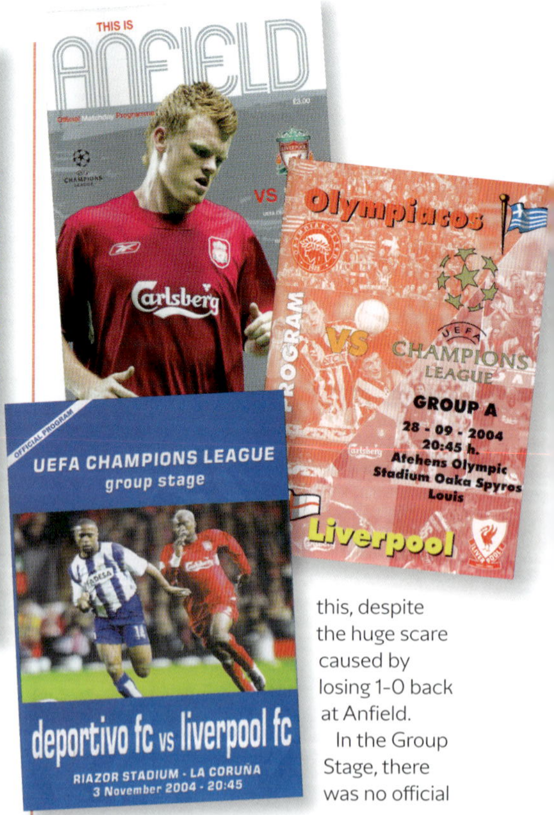

In the Group Stage, there was no official programme for the match in Greece against Olympiacos. There was an unofficial issue, which had a similar cover design to those produced in 2000/01 and is believed to originate in Spain. Similar covers were used for the Juventus and AC Milan matches later in the season. Despite being labelled as "Official Program", the Deportivo de La Coruña blue-cover edition is

UEFA Champions League
Qualifikation 3.Runde

GAK

vs.

LIEBHERR GAK - FC Liverpool

Dienstag, 10.08.2004, 20.45 Uhr
Arnold Schwarzenegger Stadion Graz-Liebenau

Schiedsrichter:
SARS Alain (FRA)

Schiedsrichterassistenten:
CHAUDRE Jean-Paul, REINBOLD Patrick (FRA)

	LIEBHERR GAK		FC LIVERPOOL
1	SCHRANZ Andreas	1	DUDEK Jerzy
4	TOKIC Mario	3	FINNAN Stephen
5	EHMANN Anton K	4	HYYPIA Sami
6	RAMUSCH Dieter	5	BAROS Milan
7	STANDFEST Joachim	7	KEWELL Harry
8	MURATOVIC Samir	8	GERRARD Steven K
10	SKORO Alen	9	CISSE Djibril
11	AMERHAUSER Martin	16	HAMANN Dietmar
18	POGATETZ Emanuel	17	GONZALEZ Jose Miguel
20	AUFHAUSER Rene	18	RIISE John
28	KOLLMANN Roland	23	CARRAGHER James
	ERSATZSPIELER		ERSATZSPIELER
ET 13	ALMER Franz	ET 21	KIRKLAND Christopher
17	PIRKER Daniel	2	HENCHOZ Stephane
19	DOLLINGER Matthias	34	POTTER Darren
22	BAZINA Mario	10	OWEN Michael
23	SICK Gernot	15	DIAO Salif
25	MAJSTOROVIC Mario	24	SINAMA Florent
26	PLASSNEGGER Gernot	28	WARNOCK Stephen
Trainer	SCHACHNER Walter	Trainer	BENITEZ Rafael

unofficial, again produced in Spain. The Todo Deporte Coruña club magazine was on sale in the stadium; it does preview the match, but cannot be considered a programme. AS Monaco issued a gatefold programme, which was only available in VIP areas. By the narrowest of margins, the Reds qualified for the knockout stage; who can fail to remember that Gerrard goal, minutes from the final whistle?

At the Round of 16 stage, Bayer 04 Leverkusen produced their usual BayArena Magazin for the second leg. For the first time since Heysel, Juventus were Liverpool's next opponents. There was no official issue for the second leg, just the aforementioned Spanish

edition, plus an Italian issue with a black cover, which has the feel of a Pockart issue and is said to have been available at the match. A black-and-white, folded A4 single sheet could also be found across bars in Turin.

The all-English semi-final against Chelsea proved to be a tight affair, with Luis García's goal separating the sides over the two legs. Note the clever use of four gold stars on the front on the programme for the second leg. Standard home programmes were issued for the home Group Stage matches and knockout stage. Istanbul hosted the final in the "out-of-the-city" Atatürk Olympic Stadium.

Other mementos of Istanbul from match tickets, newspapers and magazines to teamsheets, match guides and more

Pictured here is a range of official UEFA printed matter produced for the final. Highlighted are a pre-event pass, information guides, blue and silver welcome package brochures plus a matchday menu.

Two issues of the Forza Milan! magazine produced ahead of the final along with the English-language Calcio Italia

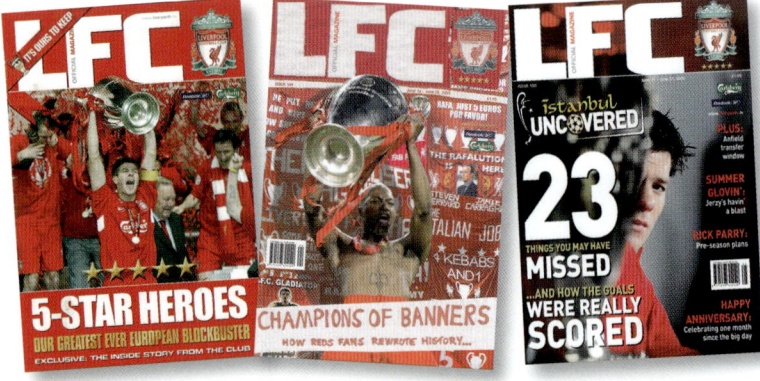

Three copies of the Official LFC Weekly magazine that were published in the weeks after the final, together with the Official Liverpool Supporters' Club publication featuring Steven Gerrard lifting the trophy

Below: an unofficial guide

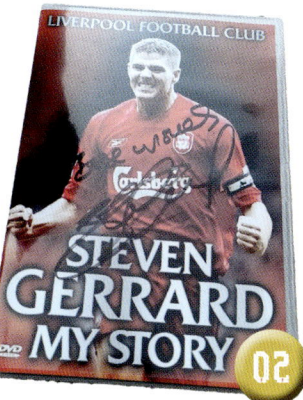

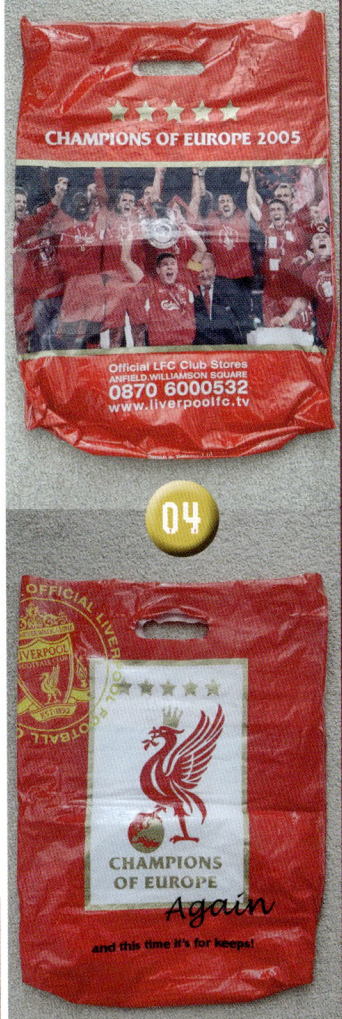

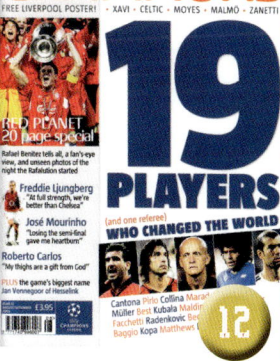

01. ON YOUR PLATE:
A collectors' dinner plate featuring the Reds' triumph

02. CAPTAIN'S TALE:
A DVD featuring Liverpool captain and Istanbul hero Steven Gerrard, signed by the man himself

03. CATALOGUE OF GOODIES:
A Champions of Europe special issue of the club's merchandise offerings, its pages packed with celebratory items - who had this duvet?

04. IN THE BAG:
The double-sided carrier bags selling merchandise at official club stores in the weeks after the final

05. READ ALL ABOUT IT:
UEFA's official match report and statistics issued to journalists after the penalty shoot-out

06. TECHNICAL TEAM:
The official 2004/05 UEFA Champions League review

07. TURKISH TAKE:
The cover of a Turkish paper the following day

08. FIVE TIMES:
The front page of The Times on 27 May 2005

09. FANATIK DAY:
An Istanbul sports newspaper prepares for the city's big night

10. FANATIK NIGHT:
The Istanbul-based publication highlights the Reds' success

11. FIFTY YEARS:
UEFA Champions Magazine supplement celebrating 50 years of the European Cup/ Champions League

12. RED PLANET:
Steven Gerrard's trophy lift features on the cover of UEFA's Champions Magazine for August/ September 2005

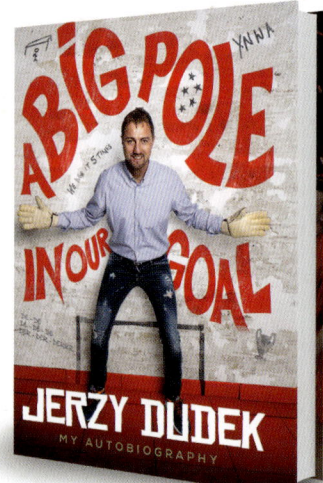

"YOU CAN WIN THIS FOR US!"

In 2016, Trinity Mirror Sport Media (now Reach Sport) published Jerzy Dudek's autobiography A Big Pole In Our Goal. In this extract the goalkeeper reflects on the drama of the penalty shoot-out in Istanbul

t was total chaos on the pitch after extra-time had finished. A combination of tiredness, tension and disbelief that we'd somehow turned the game around made this a very intense period. A couple of lads came over to me and said some words of praise: "Great work Jerzy! Now focus on the penalties. It's your game, you can win this for us!"

Carra was the most excited. He pushed me, got right into my face and shouted at me.

"Jerzy, try to do something to put them off. Do you remember Grobbelaar? Be like him, he irritated everyone in Rome! Do the wobbly legs! Move around on the goal-line! Distract them!"

"Okay Carra, okay, okay! But leave me alone, let me focus on the penalties!"

"Remember! Do something. You have to do something! Remember Grobbelaar! You have to!"

I just kept saying okay to Carra as I really wanted to speak about the penalties with Ocho, our goalkeeping coach, but I kept what he said in mind. Maybe it was worth a try.

Rafa was very keen on attention to detail and before the final all the information about AC Milan's penalty and free-kick takers was put on a board in the dressing room. There were also video clips for me to watch of their players taking penalties and set-pieces. Saving penalties is something Rafa had actually worked with me on throughout the season, his first as Liverpool manager.

"How would you describe penalties?" he said to me? "Top, low, middle? You need to look at it differently. He advised me to mentally divide the goal into six squares. Starting from the top right would be squares one, two and three and from the bottom left would be squares four, five and six. I would then look at videos of opposition penalty takers and work out which 'square' they were most likely to strike their penalty towards. It took me four months to truly get my head around it and every so often Benitez would test me. "How Lampard is shooting? Which number?" I answered "six" – the right low corner of the goal – but everyone except myself and Rafa had no clue what we were talking about. We had our own penalty code.

While we were waiting for the shoot-out, which would be taken at the end of the Ataturk Stadium where all six goals had been scored – in front of the AC Milan fans – Ocho took out a list detailing the penalty-taking habits of their player. It was written in our code with each AC Milan player having a number next to his name. It felt like that list was as long as a toilet roll!

"I'm not going to remember all this," I said to Ocho. "You need to help me." I tried to convince him to stand behind the goal to give me instructions, but obviously the referee wasn't going to allow him to do this, so I came up with another plan instead.

"Before each penalty I'm going to look at you. Stand up and raise your hands. If you raise one hand, I'll go left, if you raise two, I'll go right. That's all you can do from the distance, but it will help me."

I'm not sure if many people noticed this, but it was actually Scott Carson who would raise his hands to signal which way I would dive. Ocho would look at his notes and tell him which arm to raise as each of their players walked down towards me. But it wasn't an easy call for Ocho to make. Some players vary their penalties so I could see some consternation in Ocho's face every single time he had to make a decision on which way I should dive. It reminded me of when ski-jumping coaches have to wave a flag to signal when their ski-jumper should start his descent down the slope. He is waiting for perfect wind conditions before he waves that flag, but it's a test of nerve as to when he does so in the time allotted before a jump must be made. The ski-jumper puts his faith in his coach to make that call and that is what I did with Ocho. Scott's arms would effectively be my flag.

★★★★★

AC Milan would take their penalties first and the first man to step up was Serginho, their Brazilian winger, who had taken and scored the first penalty in their 2003 Champions League final penalty shoot-out victory against Juventus at Old Trafford. He was one of three specialist penalty takers that Carlo Ancelotti, AC Milan's coach, had on the pitch, so naturally he selected him to go first. Before he took the penalty I grabbed the ball and tried to look into his eyes. Then, as I handed it to him, I said "Same as usual, mate? You'll shoot to the same side as you usually do, right?"

I don't know if he understood me. I had no idea if he spoke English. It was just a game to try and mess with his head. Even if he didn't understand me, I wanted to confuse him by talking at him. I wanted to dominate the penalty shoot-out, to give the impression that I was in charge, even to the referee! I wanted to show the AC Milan players that I ruled on the pitch, not them or the referee. I needed to show I was confident, relaxed and make my opponents feel uncomfortable. That's why I reacted flippantly to the ref when he told me to get back onto the goal-line. 'I'll go when I'm ready, ref, I'm in charge here'.

I had spotted the signal from Scott and now I had no interest in anything else other than the ball and the shooter. Nothing else.

> "Before each penalty I'm going to look at you. Stand up and raise your hands. If you raise one hand, I'll go left, if you raise two, I'll go right"

I was focused as like never before in my life. It was like I was in a trance. After my save in extra-time it felt like I had received a shot of confidence and I also had what Carra had said to me in the back of my mind.

When Serginho placed the ball on the spot, I started to move my hands. I wanted him to pay attention to what was going on in the goal. When he looked at me, I moved. I stopped when he stopped. He looked again, so I raised my hands and started to move them like an air traffic controller waving a plane in at Istanbul Airport. Then, while he was preparing to take his run up, I moved right and left on the line. Maybe he got confused at seeing me do this. Perhaps it created uncertainty and indecision in his mind.

Usually the player knows where he wants to shoot before he steps up to take a penalty. The decision is already made. But after my antics on the goal-line I wonder if it made Serginho change his mind? As he took the kick I dived to my right as planned, but I didn't need to make a save. Serginho sliced the ball high and wide. "This is it!" I thought, "Keep it going."

Didi Hamann was our first taker. He was the most experienced player in our squad and calm in these situations. As he stepped up I wondered if Dida would try to distract our players in the same way that I was doing. Two years earlier, AC Milan had beaten Juventus on penalties in the Champions League final and Dida had saved three penalties in the shoot-out, from David Trezeguet, Marcelo Zalayeta and Paolo Montero. However, he was heavily criticised for being allowed to get away with moving a long way off his line before the kicks were taken. I don't know if he was thinking about that in Istanbul, but he stayed completely still with his arms at his side until the very last second when Didi was taking his run up.

Didi showed great composure. He struck the ball powerfully to the right of Dida, who dived that way, and it nestled in the bottom corner. One-nil for us and I knew that if I could stop the second penalty we could be in a very commanding position.

Andrea Pirlo was next. I looked towards our bench and Scott had one hand raised so I was meant to go left. I stared at Pirlo. I tried to look directly into his eyes. Then I started dancing on the line! I waved my arms, squatted down, jumped up and moved from left to right. Pirlo ran towards the ball slowly. He was trying to provoke me to dive early so he could then slot the ball to the other side, but it didn't work. As he slowly stepped forward, so did I taking a couple of steps towards him but without diving. Pirlo couldn't delay his penalty any longer and he struck the ball to my right. I dived the right way and saved the penalty (although not the way Scott had signalled!), but I'd taken so many steps by now that I was about three metres off the line!

Dida started to scream at the referee. He was demanding it

should be retaken. In that split second I thought to myself that if I looked at the ref it would be an admission of guilt, that I knew I was too far off my line and would be giving him a reason to tell Pirlo to retake the penalty. So instead I turned away from him, raised both of my arms in the air and then looked towards the AC Milan fans behind the goal. It may have looked like I was being arrogant, but that wasn't my intention.

When I turned back towards him he had allowed the penalty to stand. Dida was still furious, so as I walked past him to the part of the pitch where a goalkeeper must wait while his team-mates are taking penalties I shouted at him in English. "You did the same two years ago, don't you remember?!" He made a gesture at me. "Calm down," I said, smiling at him.

You can't beat the emotions you feel at moments like that. It doesn't even cross your mind if the other person understands you. There are so many things going on in your head but really you just want to enjoy the moment no matter how tense it is.

Djibril Cisse, who came on as a substitute for Milan Baros late in the second half, was our second taker. I'd beaten him at 10-pin bowling the day before but now I wanted to see him beat a goalkeeper with a football! Again Dida stayed still and Djibril sent him the wrong way, confidently slotting the ball low to his left. Now the attention was back on me and I really, really wanted to save the next one.

Jon Dahl Tomasson was next. He was my best mate when we played in Feyenoord. He must have taken loads of penalties against me in training in the past but he wasn't someone who always did the same thing. I tried to talk to him as I handed him the ball, but he didn't react. He was ice-cool. He didn't even look at me before he started his run up. Jon is very aggressive so I thought he might try a powerful shot, but he was also a player who could place skilful penalties into the net too. In this instance I simply had to guess which way he would choose to go. Bizarrely, as he ran up to take it, an ambulance drove past on the running track behind the goal. I wasn't aware of this at the time – it's only something that I've noticed on the replays – but even that didn't distract Jon. I dived to the left and he struck a hard shot low to the right, but fairly

> "As he slowly stepped forward, so did I taking a couple of steps towards him but without diving. Pirlo couldn't delay his penalty any longer and he struck the ball to my right"

centrally. That annoyed me. Had I dived to my right there was a good chance I would have save it, but now it was 2-1 for us with John Arne Riise up next.

'Ginge' was always one of our best penalty takers in training. He always put his foot through the ball, smashing it into the net. He never missed either and I fully expected him to extend our lead. Unfortunately the situation stressed him out. He felt under pressure. I think he lacked confidence from the past when he had taken penalties and instead of his usual powerful shot, he tried to beat Dida with a light, precise penalty low to the right. Dida saved it. It dispirited me a bit – Milan could go level at 2-2 if they scored next – but I stayed focused:

"Keep focused! Stay focused on your penalties and do your job," I said to myself. "Don't you dare to be happy with the things you have already done. What if you concede all the rest of the penalties and Dida saves his? What kind of satisfaction will you have if you saved a penalty, but lost anyway?" I'd experienced this kind of situation in the past and I know how it hurts. A goalkeeper gets praised for saving penalties in a shoot-out but it is no consolation if you lose the game.

Kaka, maybe Brazil's star player at the time, was AC Milan's fourth penalty taker. I decided it was time to copy Bruce Grobbelaar and do the 'spaghetti legs' that had put the AS Roma players off when Liverpool won the European Cup on penalties in Rome in 1984. I

> "Vladi took his penalty with great confidence. Dida dived to the right again and Vladi went left. Three-two. And that meant all the pressure was now on Milan's fifth penalty taker"

move to the left, to the right, wobbled my legs and moved forward off my line but Kaka wasn't distracted. He hit the ball high to my right as I dived to the left. Two-two. We still had a penalty in hand though and Vladimir Smicer walked forward to take it.

This was to be Vladi's last game for Liverpool. His career at Anfield hadn't quite gone as well as he had hoped it would, but he now had the opportunity to end it in the best way possible. Having come on as a substitute for Harry Kewell – the player who had been handed the number seven shirt he used to wear – he had scored in our comeback but if he now missed a penalty and we ended up losing maybe that is what he would be remembered for. I was quite surprised that Rafa selected Vladi to take a spot-kick, but then he asked all three subs to take a penalty so maybe he felt those with the freshest legs were the best contenders. Vladi took his penalty with great confidence. Dida dived to the right again and Vladi went left. Three-two. And that meant all the pressure was now on Milan's fifth penalty taker who just happened to be the man I had made my miracle save from in extra-time.

Andriy Shevchenko had won the Ballon d'Or in 2004 and had finished third in the voting for FIFA World Player of the Year. He'd also scored 26 goals in 39 games before the Champions League final and that was a worse return than he'd managed the year before! But now the pressure was on him. If he missed, or I save it, we would win

RbK

the European Cup, but I wasn't thinking of that as he walked towards me. He looked stressed, worried. Like a man with the weight of the world on his shoulders. Two years ago he had converted the penalty that won the Champions League for AC Milan in Manchester, but this was a totally different pressure. Sheva had to score to save them so it didn't surprise me that he was feeling the heat.

I had hold of the ball as he reached the penalty area and as I passed it to him I gave him something else to think about. "Andriy? Andriy? Will you shoot the same way as usual?"

As he ran up to strike the ball I danced around on the goal-line again. I waved my arms, jumped and did the wobbly legs. I think it created uncertainty in his mind as when he reached the ball he almost stopped. He wanted to shoot to my right side but at the last second he spotted that I was diving that way so tried to change his mind and put the ball in the opposite corner. But it was too late. He couldn't adjust his body and sent the ball straight down the middle.

I was hanging in the air like someone had miraculously held me there. It was like slow motion as the ball came towards me. I raised my left hand and my left leg as I dived to my right in the hope I would get something on it. The ball hit my left hand. It landed one metre in front of the goal-line. I saved it! I saved it! I SAVED IT!!!

I leapt to my feet, ran right past the referee and when I saw the rest of my team-mates running towards me the realisation that it was all over hit me. So did the lads! The other 10 players who had been lining up on the halfway line, the subs and all the rest of the squad jumped on top of me. I was lying on the ground with a pile of Liverpool players on top of me!

It was total madness, a sense of euphoria I had never experienced before and cannot accurately describe now. We had won the Champions League. We were champions of Europe. After being 3-0 behind at half-time. And I had made the crucial penalty save. It was beyond my wildest dreams!

★★★★★

While we were waiting for the presentation, Benitez came over to me on the pitch and, without displaying any emotion, said to me: "Tell me, Jerzy, why did you dive in completely different directions than we showed you?"

He was right. I think I dived at least three times in the opposite direction than I should have done according to the signals that were being made on the touchline for me from Scott and Ocho. Unlike the incredibly serene Rafa I hadn't thought of that in the midst of all the celebrations, but I'm glad I did!

10

THINGS YOU MAY HAVE MISSED
THEN

Think you've seen everything from the 2005 Champions League final?
Think again. In all the excitement we reckon you might just have missed a few things that happened on that magical night in Istanbul. And we don't mean the second half for anyone who left at half-time...

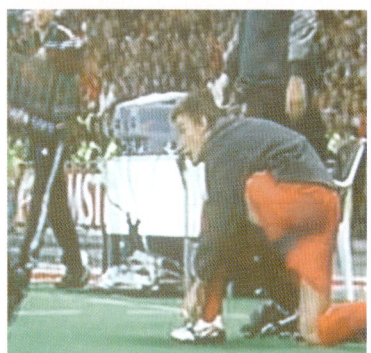

1 VLADI CAUGHT ON THE HOP
Vladimir Smicer would have made his final appearance for the Reds, as a first half substitute for the injured Harry Kewell, a little earlier than he did had the Czech international had his boots on his feet.

So confident was Vladi that he wouldn't be needed early that he was sat on the bench in his socks.

3 PAIN IN THE GUM?
When Carlo Ancelotti strolled back out of the tunnel after the half-time interval he was slowly chewing gum as he took his seat in the dugout.

After Smicer had scored Liverpool's second goal in the space of three minutes the camera focused on him and his jaw was now moving rapidly.

Whenever he was seen for the remainder of the game his chewing was always rapid which told you that Liverpool's comeback had engulfed him with nerves and fear.

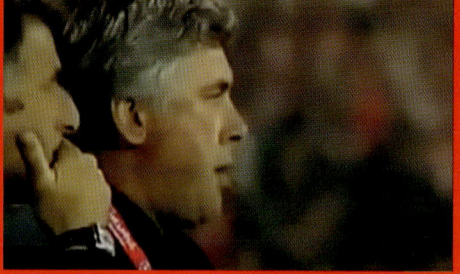

5 TAILS YOU LOSE
The Gods of fortune were uppermost in the thinking of Milan skipper Paolo Maldini when the captains were called together to toss a coin to decide which way the teams would be shooting for the first period of extra-time.

Maldini won the toss for the second time and opted to turn Liverpool around so his side were shooting the same way as they were at the start of the game when they took Liverpool apart.

There was to be no repeat showing from the Italians though.

2 KAKA'S HALF-TIME SHIRT SWAP
No-one inside the Ataturk Stadium, or watching the action in Liverpool or around the world would dispute the fact that Kaka was the main cause of Liverpool's first half discomfort.

Despite the oppressive heat of the Istanbul evening the mercurial Brazilian quite clearly had a black t-shirt on under his shirt during the first half. After half-time the black was replaced with white.

The Biblical character Samson lost his powers when his flowing locks were shorn - maybe Kaka's powers were similarly removed when he made the switch.

4 MILAN'S GOOD LUCK GESTURE
Despite his obvious disappointment at being withdrawn prematurely from the biggest game of his career, Milan Baros still took time to wish Djibril Cisse all the best when he entered the fray.

The pair shared an intimate moment on the touchline when Baros passed on some encouraging words as they stood nose to nose. They then bumped foreheads and it was Cisse's time to shine.

6 TOUCH OF RESPECT
Proving the respect both sides had for each other, Steven Gerrard and Andriy Shevchenko exchanged kind words and an embrace as the first half of extra-time drew to a close.

Both look knackered after their exertions so perhaps they were helping carry each other back towards their team-mates taking on water at the half-way line.

The pair, two of Europe's finest footballing talents, also took time for a chat at the end of extra-time too.

7 GET HERE, VLADI!

The relief which washed over the normally demure Vladimir Smicer when his penalty had found the corner of Dida's net was obvious as he ran to the Liverpool supporters closest to that end of the ground.

What was less obvious were the efforts of skipper Steven Gerrard and Jamie Carragher to get him back to the half-way line before Andriy Shevchenko took what was to be the decisive pen.

Carra broke from the Liverpool line on the halfway line to scream at his mate and Vladi finally got the message. He got back to join the huddle just in time to see Jerzy's heroics from the perfect angle - and he was promptly off celebrating again.

Luis Garcia and Carragher both volunteered for spot-kicks but were turned down by Rafa who had insisted all along that he would decide on the takers after judging the players' fitness.

Garcia looked particularly determined to take one and pleaded his case to the gaffer but his pleas fell on deaf ears. Rafa's judgement? Spot-on.

8 THREE CHEERS
FOR THE CHAMPIONS

The savage nature of their defeat obviously hurt Milan, and as the Reds began their celebrations most of Milan's players and backroom staff decided to flee the field.

Only club captain Paolo Maldini, Andriy Shevchenko and Rino Gattuso remained on the field for the entire duration of Liverpool's euphoric celebrations and you could only praise the trio for their show of sportsmanship.

They looked visibly distraught but still applauded their conquerors. When the rest of the Milan squad re-appeared, they too applauded the victors onto the winners' rostrum and shook hands and hugged the Reds.

9 DJIBRIL's JIG

As the entire Liverpool squad assembled with their medals on the podium, only Steven Gerrard had yet to set foot on the platform.

His arrival was delayed by a dancing Djibril Cisse who was doing his thing around European club football's most coveted prize. Doing his thing, that is, until Carragher intervened. You just saw a hand creep onto the television picture hauling the Frenchman back to a respectable distance as Stevie made his way towards the trophy.

10 LUCKY NETS

The European campaign had been littered with omens and superstitions. There were dying Popes, Welsh Grand Slams and a Royal Wedding to name a few.

We've got another one to add to the list. In 1981 in Paris the goal nets were black and Liverpool won. They were the same colour in Rome in 1984 too and the end result was the same - Liverpool were the Kings of Europe.

So it was too in Istanbul. 1984 saw Bruce Grobbelaar's wobbly leg antics in front of those nets and it didn't take Einstein to see where Jerzy Dudek drew inspiration for his own goal-line dance routine.

Fate aside, there was another reason Liverpool won on all those occasions. They dug deep, showed real character and deserved victory.

10

THINGS YOU MAY HAVE MISSED
SINCE

Liverpool's triumph in Turkey will go down in folklore. In the two decades since, it has produced films, stage shows and academic analysis. Here's just 10 things that have happened in the wake of Istanbul that may have passed you by...

Istanbul
2005

1 OURS TO KEEP

Liverpool's triumph marked the Reds' fifth European Cup success and the first by an English team since 1999. By winning the cup for a fifth time, Liverpool FC earned the privilege of wearing a multiple-winner badge and the right to keep the trophy (under normal competition rules, the winning club could keep the trophy for only 10 months, as they had to deliver it back to UEFA two months before the following year's final).

Liverpool were given ownership of the trophy every winner had held aloft since 1995 (after Milan were permanently awarded the previous trophy after their fifth win in 1994).

The 2005/06 participants competed for a new identical trophy. The rule to keep the trophy, which had been in effect since the 1968/69 season, was changed for the 2008/09 campaign so that the actual trophy remained with UEFA at all times.

Liverpool became the fifth and final club to be given the honour after Real Madrid, Ajax, Bayern Munich and Milan – all of whom had either won at least five times or three times consecutively.

2 DIEGO'S SALUTE

Argentina legend Diego Maradona, widely considered one of the game's all-time greats, lauded the Reds after the match.

"Even the Brazil team that won the 1970 World Cup could not have staged a comeback with Milan leading 3-0...," he said. "The English club proved that miracles really do exist. I've now made Liverpool my English team. They showed that football is the most beautiful sport of all.

"You knew they could defend, but the team showed they could play too and wrote a page in the history books. The match will last forever. The Liverpool supporters didn't let me go to sleep the night before.

"There were 10 of them to every three Milan supporters. They showed their unconditional support at half-time when they were losing 3-0 and still they didn't stop singing."

3 A PARADE IN A MILLION

Liverpool celebrated their victory by parading the trophy around the city in an open-top double-decker bus the day after the final. They were cheered by approximately 1 million supporters, with an estimated 300,000 fans located around St George's Hall opposite Lime Street Station– the final destination of the parade.

Business experts estimated that one in five workers took time off following the victory. It was also estimated that Liverpudlians drank around 10,000 bottles of champagne after the match, with supermarket chain Sainsbury's stating: "We've never seen anything like it. We would usually expect to sell this much champagne at Christmas."

4 CASE FOR THE DEFENCE

Despite winning the competition, Liverpool's place in the following season's Champions League was initially in doubt. Prior to the 2005 UEFA Champions League final, The Football Association had decided on 5 May that only the top four finishers in the Premier League would qualify and Liverpool ended their domestic season in fifth place behind Everton.

UEFA initially maintained that each country could only have four Champions League spots and suggested that the FA could nominate Liverpool instead of Everton. Can you imagine!

Liverpool faced a three-week wait to discover if they would be allowed to defend their title as all previous winners of the competition had done. UEFA came to a decision on 10 June, confirming that both Everton and Liverpool would be able to compete in the Champions League; however, Liverpool were entered into the first qualifying round and were given no 'country protection' - meaning they could have faced another English club at any stage of the competition, later drawn with Chelsea in the group stage.

The UEFA Executive Committee also amended the regulations for future competitions so that the holders would have the right to defend their title and therefore qualify automatically, though at the expense of the lowest placed team in countries that had more than one qualifier.

5 SUPER CUP AND CLUB WORLD CHAMPIONSHIP

As champions, Liverpool faced CSKA Moscow (winners of the 2005 UEFA Cup final) in the 2005 UEFA Super Cup, held on 26 August with the Reds winning 3-1 after extra time.

Liverpool's victory in Istanbul also meant they qualified for the 2005 FIFA Club World Championship. Rafa Benitez's men beat Deportivo Saprissa 3-0 in the semi-final, and played Copa Libertadores champions São Paulo in the final, somehow losing 1-0.

6 STAGE SHOWS AND MOVIES

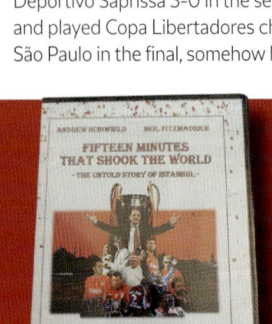
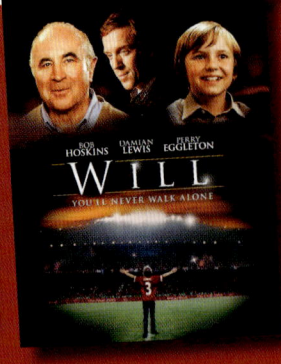
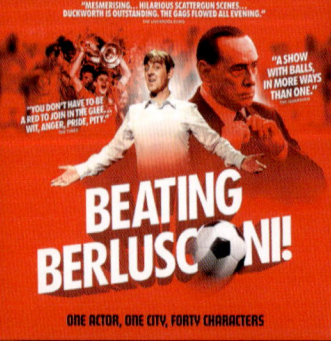

The Reds' remarkable triumph was the inspiration behind several theatre productions and films.

Fifteen Minutes That Shook the World, One Night in Istanbul, Beating Berlusconi and Will all made stage or screen, while the game was also an important shared memory between the main characters of the 2017 Korean romantic drama TV series Rain or Shine.

7 JERZY BOY

In a 2011 poll conducted by UEFA.com, Jerzy Dudek's double save from Andriy Shevchenko in the 117th minute was voted the greatest Champions League moment of all time, ahead of Zinedine Zidane's left-footed volley against Bayer Leverkusen in the 2002 final and Ole Gunnar Solskjær's injury-time winner against Bayern Munich in 1999 for Manchester United.

When asked to explain his saves after the game, an emotional Dudek said he took inspiration from Pope John Paul II (a fellow Pole and goalkeeper in his youth) who died in April, the month before the final. "I'm dedicating this to the memory of John Paul. I had contact with him during his life and I've felt the inspiration since his death. I can't account for it."

Dudek dubbed it the 'Hand of Pope', an allusion to Diego Maradona dubbing his infamous first goal in the 1986 World Cup quarter final the 'Hand of God'.

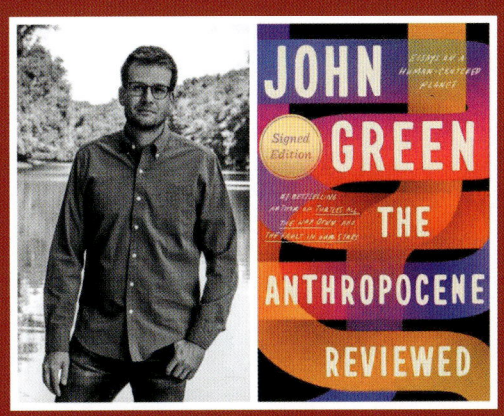

8 ANTHROPOCENE ANALYSIS

The final is discussed in author John Green's podcast The Anthropocene Reviewed, and the essay was later adapted for Green's book of the same name. The podcast is said to review 'different facets of the human-centered planet on a five-star scale'.

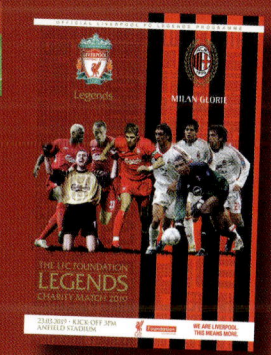

9 ISTANBUL 2.0

Many of the men who played in the 2005 final also played for their clubs' legends teams, Liverpool Legends and Milan Glorie, in Liverpool's 2019 Legends Game at Anfield.

Robbie Fowler and Djibril Cisse put Liverpool 2-0 up before Andrea Pirlo and Giuseppe Pancaro brought Milan level. Steven Gerrard then scored in the final minute of play to give Liverpool a 3-2 win. The match raised an estimated £1 million for the LFC Foundation.

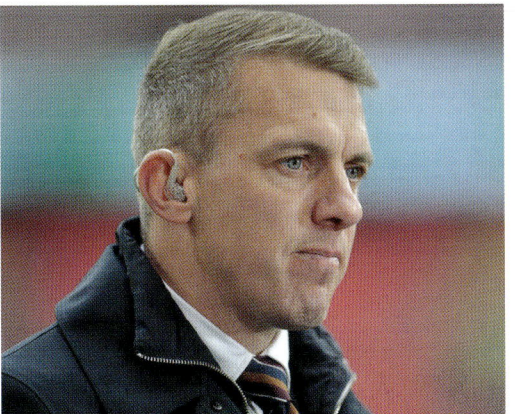

10 CHAMPION LEAGUE EXPERTISE

Stephen Warnock's Liverpool debut came in the opening game of the Reds' run to glory in 2004/05.

Warnock made his bow in the opening leg of the qualifying round game at Grazer AK.

Fast forward 20 years and the former Liverpool left-back is an integral part of the BBC's UEFA Champions League highlights coverage, being given the title 'Champions League analyst' by the corporation.

MILAN MEMORIES

How defenders Paolo Maldini and Massimo Oddo look back on the 2005 final

n 2019 the captain of the vanquished Milan side spoke to the official Liverpool FC matchday programme ahead of the charity fixture at Anfield between Liverpool FC Legends and Milan Glorie at Anfield.

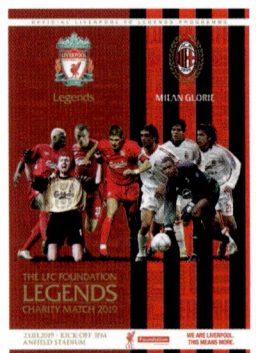

Back then the legendary Paolo Maldini recalled: "There have only been two competitive games between AC Milan and Liverpool – both in the European Cup final! – that says a lot about these two clubs.

AC Milan and Liverpool FC are two of the most important club sides at an international level. It was incredible to challenge each other twice in three seasons, and most of all, in two UEFA Champions League finals and that is due to the great qualities of both clubs.

"The knockout in Istanbul was incredible! We dominated 110 out of the 120 minutes and we created chances to score even after the 3-3 but that's football, actually that's sport. I think it was the worst moment, one of the most insane games. I remember Liverpool fans' singing, they continued to support their team even when they were losing 3-0. When penalties arrived, in our heart we knew we had already lost."

Fellow full-back Massimo Oddo had been at AC Milan between 1993 and 1999 but was a Lazio player at the time of the 2005 final. He rejoined the Rossoneri in January 2007 and played in the 2007 final against the Reds as they gained revenge with a 2-1 win in Athens. He also played for Milan Glorie in the Legends game at Anfield six years ago.

He reflected: "Winning the Champions League is the top trophy for a club and it is not a given nor is it easy to raise that cup to the heavens. It is incredible and everything around it is incredible. You can feel and breathe the importance of the event a lot before the kick-off so there are many great moments before and after a triumph like that. We are talking of emotions that get even stronger

with time because on the day of a match like that, you don't really figure out what you're going to face, but the importance of the event is even bigger when you watch it afterwards and the emotions you feel today are even bigger when you watch the images, when you see what happened. You realise what happened right now more than on the day of the match."

STILL SINKING IN!

Twenty years on: how those who played in the 2005 UEFA Champions League final remember what happened

RAFAEL BENITEZ
"We knew how we could come back from the dead"

"These are the moments that measure you as a manager. The times when the players have lost faith, when their confidence is shattered, their belief washed away in a tide of embarrassment, disappointment and regret. These are the moments when all the work you have done over the course of a season, a career, bears its reward.

"Those players who stood at the centre of that vast bowl, watched by 50,000 Liverpool fans, had not been sent back onto that pitch [after half-time] instructed to limit the damage or avoid further humiliation. They had not been allowed to think that all was lost. Half-time offered us just 15 minutes to convince them that there was hope, however distant; that there was a chance, however slim. We did all we could to show them that there was a way, that there was no reason to give up, to prove to them that we had a plan. And after all that had happened in that dispiriting first half, they believed.

"It would be too much to say that we had planned to score three goals in six minutes. We knew, though, that if we could score the first goal of the second half, we stood a chance. We would be back in the game.

"If we scored first, I had told the players, anything could happen. We knew that we could stop Milan, that we could right what went wrong in the first half. And we knew that we could hurt them too. We knew how we could come back from the dead."

JAMIE CARRAGHER
"One of the greatest finals of all time"

"It is one of the greatest finals of all time. People will be talking about that game in 20 or 30 years' time. It sounds strange, but I didn't really celebrate in the changing-room [immediately after the final].

"I just can't believe how we won that cup. We had a similar scenario a few years before in the FA Cup final against Arsenal [in 2001] when we were dead and buried but ended up coming back and we did it again in Istanbul.

"I was going out there in the second-half hoping that we weren't really going to embarrass ourselves more by letting in four or five.

"We didn't want it to be remembered as a final where there was a bit of an embarrassment. They got the early goal and we seemed to be pushing for the equaliser too early and they kept hitting us on the break. Jerzy's save from Shevchenko at the end of extra-time was unbelievable.

"I was just waiting for it to hit the net and it being game up. I couldn't believe it never went in and I think that was the moment that I thought our name was on the cup.

"I don't think that final will ever be bettered. We have won the trophy again since, but I think it's the way we won it that makes it so special."

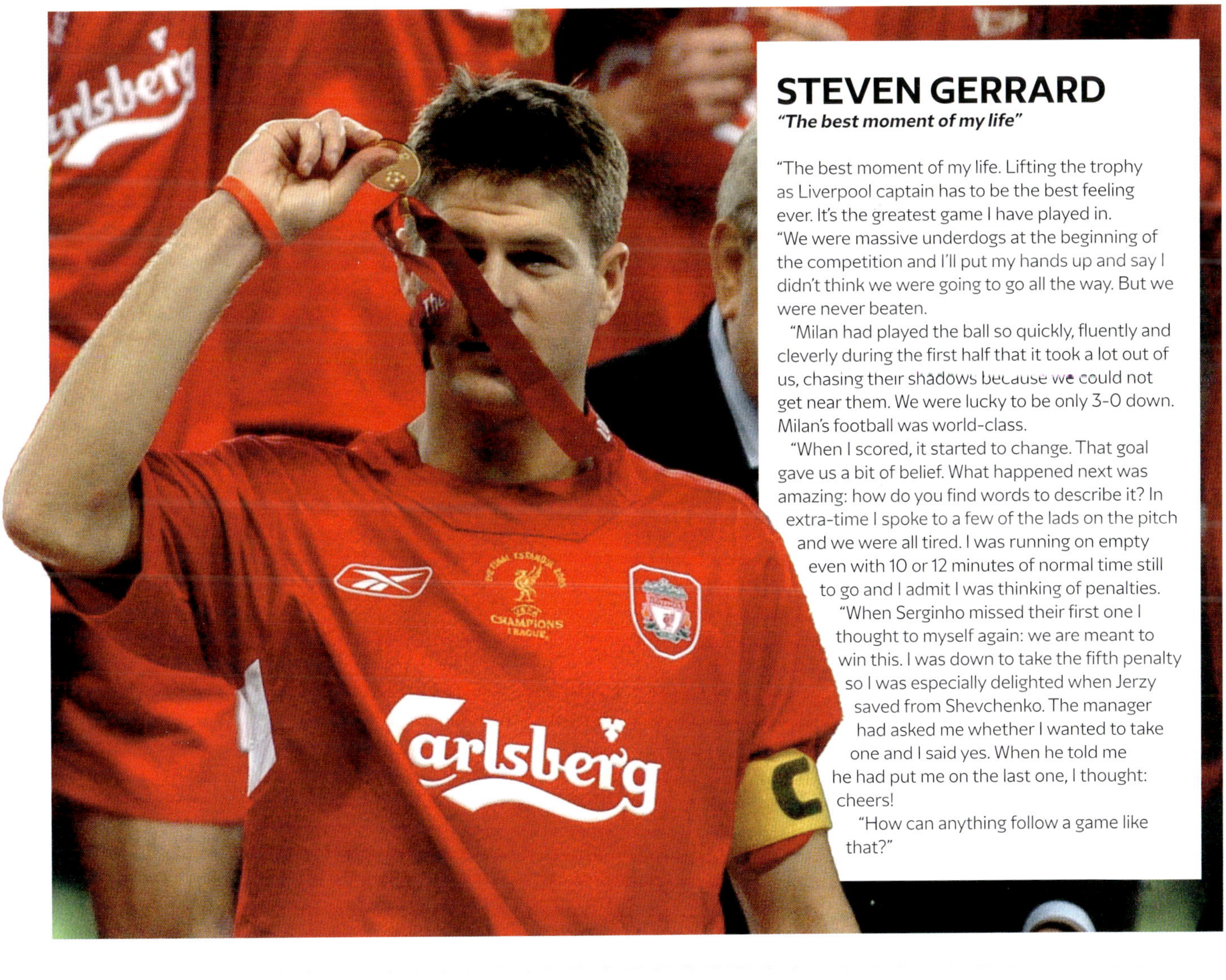

STEVEN GERRARD
"The best moment of my life"

"The best moment of my life. Lifting the trophy as Liverpool captain has to be the best feeling ever. It's the greatest game I have played in.

"We were massive underdogs at the beginning of the competition and I'll put my hands up and say I didn't think we were going to go all the way. But we were never beaten.

"Milan had played the ball so quickly, fluently and cleverly during the first half that it took a lot out of us, chasing their shadows because we could not get near them. We were lucky to be only 3-0 down. Milan's football was world-class.

"When I scored, it started to change. That goal gave us a bit of belief. What happened next was amazing: how do you find words to describe it? In extra-time I spoke to a few of the lads on the pitch and we were all tired. I was running on empty even with 10 or 12 minutes of normal time still to go and I admit I was thinking of penalties.

"When Serginho missed their first one I thought to myself again: we are meant to win this. I was down to take the fifth penalty so I was especially delighted when Jerzy saved from Shevchenko. The manager had asked me whether I wanted to take one and I said yes. When he told me he had put me on the last one, I thought: cheers!

"How can anything follow a game like that?"

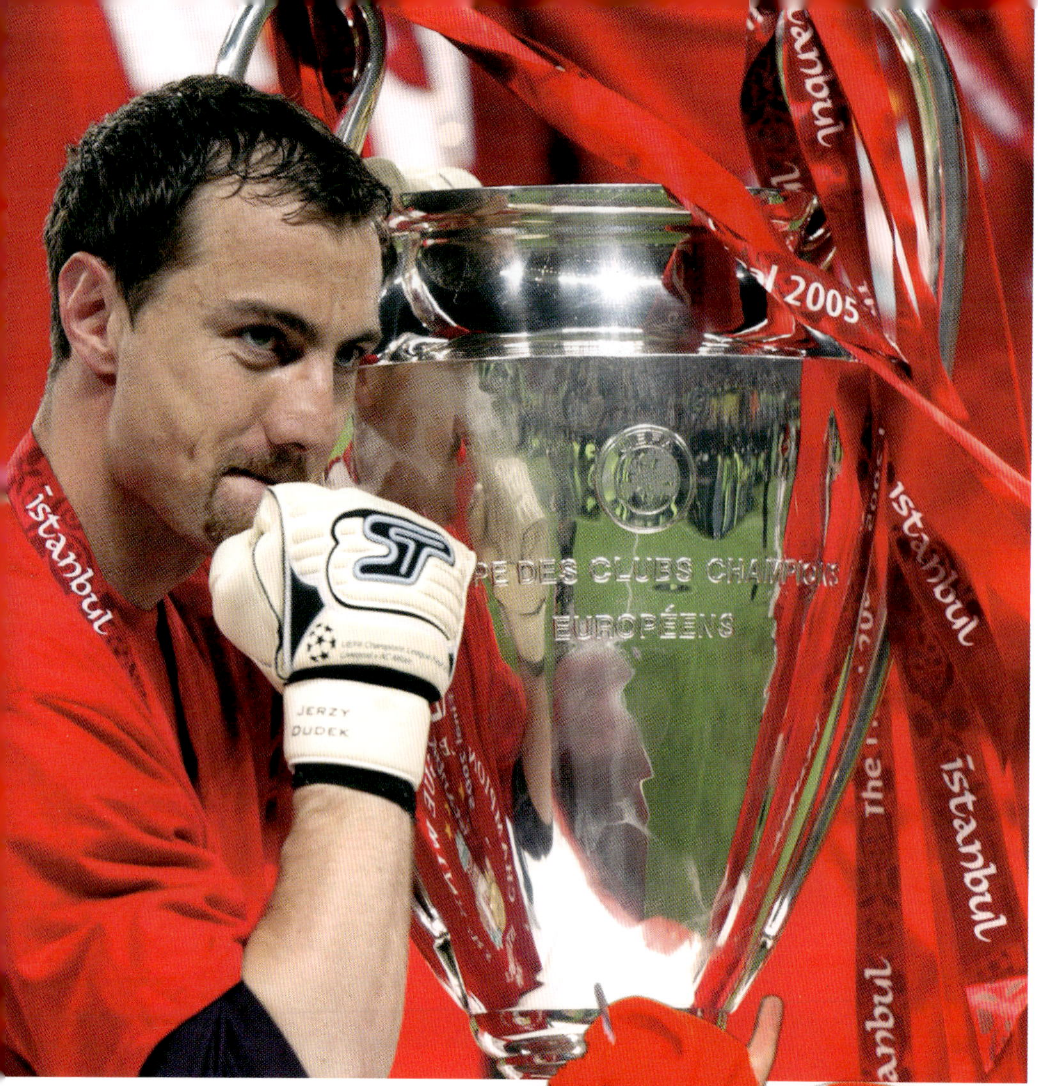

JERZY DUDEK
"We were in heaven"

"I still don't know how I did it. With that save [from Shevchenko's shot] in the last three minutes, someone up there saved us. Before the penalties Carragher came up to me like he was crazy, as always. He grabbed me and said: 'Jerzy, Jerzy, Jerzy, remember Bruce [Grobbelaar]. He did some crazy things to put them off and you have to do the same. Just put them off all the time!' He told me I would be the hero. I said: 'Okay, calm down. I've seen the video of Bruce and the penalty shoot-out loads of times'.

"The first one was missed and I saved the second. Then I tried the crazy legs for the fourth one but he [Kaka] scored. But a lot of other things worked out. It was the biggest game of all of our lives. We were in heaven afterwards."

XABI ALONSO
"It was so exciting for everybody"

"I look at the medal now and again. It's kept in a drawer, not on show, but I know exactly where it is. It was my first medal and in terms of cups it's the biggest you can win.

"Before the game Rafa told us that someone else other than Stevie would take the penalties, so when we got one [to make it 3-3 on the night] I decided that I would take it. I missed the first chance and then luckily the second one went in. I didn't have time to think about the miss as it all happened so fast.

"In fact I can remember thinking that we should have had another penalty as I felt Alessandro Nesta fouled me when I went for the rebound. That was the first thing in my mind then I saw the ball hit the roof of the net and it didn't matter anymore. I just reacted as quickly as possible and it went in to make it 3-3.

"To be 3-0 down against one of the biggest clubs in Europe and then to be back on level terms within just six minutes was incredible. It all happened so quickly and was so exciting for everybody. Us, the supporters, everybody."

JOHN ARNE RIISE
"I had cramp before my penalty"

"It was the first time really that any of us had played in this kind of big game. We tried to do everything as normal as we always did before a game, but it was hard because the build-up was in the press, on TV and everywhere, and we wanted to give that bit extra for the fans.

"I had cramp before my penalty [in the shoot-out] and I was thinking of blasting it but I was scared of getting my cramp back.

"I didn't notice [Milan goalkeeper] Dida had gone the same side for every penalty before me. I think I hit it quite well, but he just got a hand on it. Stevie Gerrard came up and gave me a pat on the back. At that time you think the worst, but it didn't take long to turn to happiness. Afterwards I was down in my underpants because I gave everything to the fans."

MILAN BAROS
"The best night in my football career"

"The greatest game I have ever played in - especially considering we were 3-0 down at half-time and still managed to win. It was a special night and I think it was my best night in my football career. I spent three-and-a-half-years at Liverpool and won the Champions League. Liverpool will always stay in my heart."

109

LUIS GARCIA
"We kept believing in ourselves"

"The fans stayed with us. They were there, even when we looked out of it, and that is something that will live with me for a very long time.

"We were all a little worried at half-time when we were 3-0 down because it didn't look as if there was any way back for us. But we kept believing in ourselves and I think we deserved to win. We showed our strengths many times that season and it was a fantastic moment for us all. It was reward for all the hard work we put in that season."

STEVE FINNAN
"I was inside the dressing-room when I heard the sound of the first goal"

"It's incredible to think it's been 20 years. It just goes to show how quickly time goes!

"I felt a bit of an injury in the first-half. You never want to come off, but it was the right decision because I wouldn't have lasted long. I was actually inside the dressing-room when I heard the sound of the first goal. You could tell the difference between the fans, so you knew it was us who scored. The comeback wasn't something you'd expect with the way the first half went, but it was surreal. That's why I moved to Liverpool.

"I guess I was a bit fortunate reaching two finals [2005 and 07] in my first three seasons in the Champions League. And that's why I have to give Rafa Benitez credit for what he can get out of a team – he was suited to that type of football and knockout competition."

DJIMI TRAORE
"I'm very proud"

"I achieved something few players ever will. I know I was not the best [player at Liverpool at the time] but I certainly tried my hardest and I'm very proud because winning the Champions League is not something everyone gets to do."

DJIBRIL CISSE
"It could only happen at Liverpool"

"This sort of fairy story could only happen at Liverpool. Only at a club with such a glorious European pedigree. Coming from three-nil down to beat AC Milan in the 2005 Champions League final was the greatest moment of my career and nothing can ever top it. What we achieved that night in Istanbul was incredible. On reflection I don't know how we managed it, but we did."

SAMI HYYPIA
"Even the neutrals will remember it forever"

"Even the neutrals will remember it forever because to come back from 3-0 down against AC Milan and then go on to win it is an incredible result.

"Even in a normal game this would be special, so for it to happen in the Champions League final makes it even more so. It will stay in the memories of the players and the fans for the rest of our lives.

"Every player dreams of winning the Champions League at some time in their career, or even just to be in the final, and I have managed to play in the final and win it – so Istanbul is definitely a highlight of my life and I think from a fan point-of-view the way the game went made it even more special."

VLADIMIR SMICER
"I lit a huge cigar!"

"When I got back to the hotel I lit a huge cigar! It is the tradition in America when you've won a trophy. I had it all night and I kept puffing and lighting it up and it never went out. I did not get any sleep at all.

"I'm so glad I scored. I always felt I owed Liverpool because I had plenty of injuries and I wanted to show the fans I am a good player. That was my seventh trophy with Liverpool. That's not bad is it?"

DIETMAR HAMANN
"The pressure of taking a penalty never worried me"

"I was always confident – about taking my penalty in the shoot-out, that is. Rafa asked if I wanted [to take] one and I nodded. From that moment on I wasn't aware of what was happening around me. I don't know who the boss spoke to, or who didn't volunteer.

"I've heard that Luis Garcia wanted one but Rafa wouldn't let him. I must ask Luis about that. But I was, as they say, in the zone – completely focused on my job. Rafa came around again and told me I'd be going first. Because I was so focused I didn't know who was next.

"I was like a supporter looking to see who was stepping up each time.

"Regardless of which penalty you are taking, I always felt the most important thing was to commit. I never thought: 'I just need to hit the target'.

"Instead I decided where I was going to hit the ball and went for it. The pressure of taking a penalty never worried me."

HARRY KEWELL
"Jerzy's double-save was unbelievable"

"The players were absolutely brilliant. From Stevie leading us, to Jamie and Sami at the back and Jerzy in goal, everyone was absolutely brilliant. The whole team was strong and we deserved to win.

"Coming towards the end of extra-time, Jerzy pulled off an absolutely magnificent double save. It was unbelievable.

"He has always been good at saving penalties, so we were hoping it would go that way because the players were getting tired and we knew what Jerzy could do. He was great. We hadn't really practised penalties before the game.

"We'd taken a few in training every now and then, but it's not something we sat down and talked about."